Lord,
KEEP YOUR MANSIONS—
JUST
Save
MY CHILDREN

RICHARD W. O'FFILL

REVIEW AND HERALD® PUBLISHING ASSOCIATION
HAGERSTOWN, MD 21740

Other books by Richard W. O'Ffill:
Expect Great Things
Transforming Prayer

To order, call 1-800-765-6955.
Visit us at www.reviewandherald.com for information on
other Review and Herald® products.
If you would like to communicate with the author
directly, please visit his Web site: www.revivalsermons.org.

Copyright © 2002 by
Review and Herald® Publishing Association
All rights reserved

The author assumes full responsibility for the accuracy of
all facts and quotations as cited in this book.

This book was
Edited by Richard W. Coffen
Copyedited by Jan Schleifer and James Cavil
Interior designed by Tina Ivany
Cover photos: Man and Boy by Photo Disc,
                   Column by © Image Ideas Ink/Picture Quest
Cover designed by Square One Design
Electronic makeup by Shirley M. Bolivar
Typeset: 10/14 Bookman

PRINTED IN U.S.A.

06 05 04 03 02   5 4 3 2 1

R&H Cataloging Service
O'Ffill, Richard Wesley, 1940-
    Lord, keep your mansions—just save my children.

    1. Parenting. 2. Spiritual life. I. Title.

            306.874

ISBN 0-8280-1670-4

THIS BOOK IS DEDICATED TO
MY CHILDREN AND GRANDCHILDREN.
I'M THANKFUL THAT GOD HAS GIVEN THEM TO ME,
FOR IT HAS BEEN THROUGH LOVING THEM
THAT I'VE LEARNED THE MEANING OF THE LOVE OF GOD.

CONTENTS

PROLOGUE

Benjamin Franklin said in *Poor Richard's Almanack:* "To err is human, to repent divine, to persist devilish." I've boiled the concept down: "To err is human; not to admit it is dumb." What we term as trial and error is really experience. Life is an ongoing experience, and what we learn as we go along is up to us. But one thing is for sure—we cannot live our lives over again.

Although we cannot live our lives over again, what life amounts to today is the sum of all our yesterdays. What life will be tomorrow depends on what we do today with those yesterdays.

At one stage in my life, my career meant everything. Next, I found myself in the acquisition stage—I wanted to own a house in the country; more was better. While I was passing through those stages, we were raising four children. Now the children are grown and have children of their own. I still have my career, and I once owned a house in the country. But now my perspective of what's important has changed.

One day as I was praying for our children and grandchildren, I said (and I hope I was not disrespectful or sacrilegious), "Lord, You have gone to prepare a mansion for me, and I've read You also have crowns. That's OK, but You can keep Your mansions and Your crowns. What I really want is for You to save my children."

I'm sure I always wanted Him to do that, but through the years my career and the material things of life were in the mix. Now nothing else matters. What I want from having lived this life is for our children—and grandchildren—to be saved.

This book is for parents and grandparents. (Singles can

profit from it if they'll learn from our experience!) As you read this book, we'll look back, we'll examine the present, and we'll look to the future. But you'll notice that this book isn't so much about our children as it is about us. Maybe I shouldn't say that it's about *you,* but it surely is about *me.* It's about feelings of guilt, frustration, even anger and grief. If that were all there was, this book would only make matters worse. But as you read, you'll also find hope, forgiveness, trust, comfort, and love. At least I hope you find those things while reading this book.

Abraham Lincoln has been attributed as saying, "You can fool all the people some of the time and some of the people all the time, but you cannot fool all the people all the time." I have my take on this one, too: "We can fool some of the people all the time, and we can fool ourselves some of the time, but we can't fool God anytime."

This book challenges us to take an honest look at ourselves in the light of some of the things we go through as parents and grandparents. What you'll read isn't always positive or affirming, but I hope that in the end it brings things together in such a way that if we'll be honest with ourselves and with God we'll discover we can be invigorated and strengthened to face the challenges of today. As we do so with increasing success, we'll have hope for tomorrow. This book doesn't attempt to deny reality or mask it, but its chapters will offer comfort, and encourage us to keep on keeping on.

Before I sat down to write, I informed our children of what I intended to do and asked their permission to proceed. They have given me that permission. The one who was the prodigal of this story said, "Dad, after all I put you and Mom through, this is the least I can do." Bless his heart.

Inasmuch as this book is about our most precious "possessions"—our children—you can imagine that as I wrote and remembered, tears often welled up in my eyes. The illustrations used are taken from real life—ours. As you read each chapter, I'm sure you'll be able to supply other illustrations from the experiences of your own life. Often we aren't aware that others are bearing burdens similar to our own. Our burdens can become much lighter if we heed the words of Scripture: "Wherefore comfort yourselves together, and edify one another, even as also ye do" (1 Thess. 5:11).

By the way, I've written not as a clinical counselor but as a person who wants to share some experiences as well as lessons learned through the application of scriptural principles. If someone were to ask me why I wrote this book, I would answer that I wrote it to give hope, encouragement, and help to others who have passed through or are passing through similar experiences.

At the end of each chapter is a section I've titled "Consider These Things." It highlights points or principles made in the chapter. There's also an interactive portion called "Discuss With Someone." Scripture says, "Iron sharpeneth iron; so a man sharpeneth the countenance of his friend" (Prov. 27:17). Sharing together sharpens our thinking and helps us broaden our horizons. Each chapter then closes with a short prayer.

It's my desire that your commitment to our heavenly Father will have deepened as a result of reading this book. And when Jesus comes in the clouds of heaven and asks, "Where is your flock, your beautiful flock?" (see Jer. 13:20) I pray that the response will be "Here we are!"

ONE

YOU ARE NOT ALONE

"To understand your parents' love, you must raise children yourself."—Chinese proverb.

It was New Year's Eve. I was sitting in the Florida room, our screened-in back porch. Although it was December 31, the weather was mild. While others were preparing to celebrate, I was hoping the year would hurry up and come to an end, because for me it had been the worst year of my life. Our youngest son was on drugs. We'd sought counsel and were told we should confront him and tell him we knew he was an addict. We did that. I also talked with anyone and everyone, and read several publications on the problem, but things weren't getting better. I had reached the end of my rope.

Now, sitting in the darkness, I began to cry. I couldn't stop. I felt all alone. As I wept, I suddenly thought of an organization called Al-Anon Family Groups. They're like Narcotics Anonymous but offer support for the families of addicts. In the phone book I located the telephone number of an Alcoholics Anonymous (AA) chapter. I called and told them I needed to attend an Al-Anon meeting. The voice at the other end of the line was kind and understanding. The person asked where I lived and gave me the address of a nearby meeting.

My wife, unlike me, suffers in silence; I suffer out loud! In a later chapter I share what effect the experiences of raising our children and grandchildren have had on our marriage, but suffice it to say here that she didn't see what good it would do to attend an Al-Anon meeting, although she agreed to go with me for my sake.

We found a local chapter that had convened in a church not far from where we lived, and we went that very New Year's Eve. When we located the room, we entered shyly. All sat around a table and introduced themselves. I said, "My name is Dick." Everyone else replied, "Hi, Dick." The meeting lasted an hour, and I didn't say anything more, because I cried the whole time. Although each Al-Anon chapter meets only once a week, I discovered that there were other meetings at locations all over the city, and I tried to go to one every night. Slowly but surely I began to feel better, because I realized I wasn't alone.

When you sit around a table with a dozen or more people who are suffering just as you are, it may not make the problem go away, but little by little it becomes more bearable. One person said, "When I attend this meeting, it's as though there's a giant battery in the middle of the table. When I come in the door, I plug in and sit down. When I leave, I feel I've been recharged."

There's always a special dynamic around the table. We don't sit there and tell what is going on at home. We don't need to hear more about that. We come to hear what each of us is doing about it, how we're coping with it, and how we're surviving in spite of it.

Someone has said that life is 10 percent what happens to us and 90 percent how we react. Often we exert all our energy and emotions trying to change what's happening to us, but that only makes the 90 percent more difficult. That was what had happened to me that New Year's Eve.

I'd been trying every trick in the book to get our son to

quit taking drugs and put his life back together. He'd been expelled from school and replaced as senior class president. We'd been able to work around that with correspondence courses, and somehow got him through high school graduation. He even went on to college. At that point the drug abuse was mostly steroids—at least, as far as we knew—but trying to control the problem was taking its toll. He'd say he was going to stop abusing, and then it would begin again. It had become a real emotional roller coaster. The problem was that I flew the white flag before he did!

That night when I'd first attended an Al-Anon meeting, I began to focus on the 90 percent factor, and from that moment things began to get better for me. The problem didn't go away. In fact, it would continue for 10 years and become far more complicated than it had been on that December night. But at least I'd now be ready for it. That night I discovered I was in good company. I say "good company" because as the weeks, months, and years would pass, my wife and I became aware that in one way or another there's not a family that isn't affected by some kind of grief.

The experience of having a prodigal son radically changed my life. I had been an idealist, looking for perfect people. That's changed; now I'm looking for survivors. You see, "there hath no temptation taken you but such as is common to man: but God is faithful, who will not suffer you to be tempted above that ye are able; but will with the temptation also make a way to escape, that ye may be able to bear it" (1 Cor. 10:13).

In plain English this text says that so far we've faced no trial that is not in some way common to everybody else, and we can depend on God to allow us not to be tested more than we can endure. When trials come, He will give us the strength to get through them.

An old song is titled "Nobody Knows the Trouble I've Seen." While those words have been the cry of our hearts from time to time, it would probably be more accurate to say, "Sooner or later everybody will know the trouble I've seen—that is, if they don't already know by experience."

We have the custom of greeting each other with the words "How are you?"

The stock reply is "I'm fine."

Such a response may not be exactly the truth, but it's what you're supposed to say. The exchange is sometimes called phatic speech, a kind of communication that helps form a bond, weak though it may be, between individuals. The question and response reveal friendliness and aren't trying to exchange information, as a physician might be if he or she asked a similar question.

In recent years when someone has asked me, "How are you?" I've wanted to cry out, "Can I really tell you?" But by that time we've passed in the hall, each of us weighed down with the burdens we carry and, in many cases, carry alone.

When people explain how thankful they are that their children are all in the church and what wonderful families their children have, I rejoice with them because the Bible says we should rejoice with those who rejoice (Rom. 12:15). I wish I could say the same thing when asked such a question, but for the present it's not us.

Many parents must cope with the lifelong burden of dealing with disadvantaged children. If God can give the grace and strength to raise and relate to children who have Down's syndrome or cerebral palsy, can't He give me the grace and strength to bear the sorrows of drug addiction and divorce? The promise is yes, He can. My wife and I can testify that He can. We aren't perfect, but we can be survivors.

We're not the first ones to carry a burden for our children.

It has been this way with parents from the beginning. The first parent was God Himself, the model parent. He did everything the way it's supposed to be done, yet one day a confrontation erupted in the family of heaven, and before it was over fully a third of His heavenly children turned against Him.

After that came Adam and Eve. It wasn't long before these new children were hiding in the bushes—just as all disobedient sons or daughters try to conceal themselves from their parents when they've done wrong.

These first children, who so badly disappointed their heavenly Parent, saw their first child, Cain, become the first murderer and "leave the church" forever. (I said we are in good company.)

There was once a grown son. His name was Edson. His mother was one of the founders of our church. She was in Australia when he wrote to her: "I am not at all religiously inclined" (Arthur L. White, *Ellen G. White* [Hagerstown, Md.: Review and Herald Pub. Assn., 1983], vol. 4, p. 94). This after he had for years been active in the church, working with hymnbook preparation, Sabbath school lessons, and the publishing work. The letter nearly crushed her.

The words Ellen White wrote in reply are the cry of all parents whose children are no longer in the church: "You are no more a child. I would that you were. I would cradle you in my arms, watch over you as I have done. But you are a man grown" (*ibid.*, p. 96).

When we were passing through the worst of our experiences, I remember thinking, *What happened to the little boy I once knew? What happened to the little boy who, when he was 2 years old, would climb onto my back, and we'd go into the swimming pool together?* I **remember** looking at pictures of him during those early years and feeling I'd actually lost a child.

It's not hard to look back now, because I know how it

turned out. But I've been forever changed by the experience. I sometimes tell the congregation when I preach that when the children were young I used to have a sermon titled "The Ten Commandments for Raising Children." As the years passed and my youngsters entered their early teens, I decided to change the title to "Ten Suggestions for Raising Children." After nearly 40 years of being a parent, and now as a grandparent of eight grandchildren, I call that sermon "Ten Questions I Have About How to Raise Children."

It used to be that when someone would ask me to pray for their children, I'd pat them on the shoulder and say, "My friend, I'll do that." Although I was sincere, I felt nothing. Now when someone with tears requests, "Please pray for my children," we weep together.

Do I believe it was God's plan that we'd have a prodigal son, that we'd spend five years raising a granddaughter, and that divorce would ravage the homes of most of our children? No. This has been the work of the enemy. Yet through it all God has given us strength and grace, and I believe I'm closer to Him now than I could possibly have been before.

More than once people have come to me and said, "Pastor O'Ffill, we've heard what you're going through. You're such an encouragement to us." This is no credit to my wife or me, but it is a credit to the God we serve. When we get to heaven, if you were to ask me how life on earth had been, I'd have to say that at times it was a nightmare. But I'll thank Jesus forever, because through all our tears He's brought us closer to Him than we could ever have imagined.

Second Corinthians 1:3, 4 says it just right: "Blessed be God, even the Father of our Lord Jesus Christ, the Father of mercies, and the God of all comfort; who comforteth us in all our tribulation, that we may be able to comfort them which are in any trouble, by the comfort wherewith we ourselves are comforted of God."

When we were young we used to say, "It takes one to know one." This is especially true when you're a parent whose prayer is "Lord, keep Your mansions—just save my children." It takes a parent who has been through sorrow to comfort those who are going through it. The time has come for us to stand up and not be afraid to be counted. We are not in bad company. As long as we must hang, let's hang together!

Great men and women of God from the beginning of time have had prodigal sons and daughters. The reality is that the majority of God's children have children who have wandered away. Many have believed this couldn't happen to them, or that it shouldn't be happening, or that if it were happening it should be kept covered up. I'm glad it hasn't happened to everybody, but it has happened to most of us, and the question we now have to face is What are we going to do about it?

Those who work with contagious diseases must take precautions lest they contract such diseases and themselves become victims. We must not forget that though we are parents, we are also children—God's children. And as we work and pray for the salvation of the children He has given us, we must be careful that we honor our heavenly Father and don't allow ourselves to catch the very disease we're trying to correct in our loved ones, ending up bitter, resentful, angry, or discouraged. In the chapters that follow we'll discuss the feelings that arise when our children wander from the Lord, and what we can do about them.

CONSIDER THESE THINGS

1. There are few, if any, families who are not suffering.
2. How we react to life is more important than what happens to us.
3. Even perfect parents have children who leave the Lord.

4. Trials and sufferings can actually serve to bring us closer to Jesus.
5. People who have had similar experiences can strengthen each other.

DISCUSS WITH SOMEONE

1. How can suffering bring us closer to Jesus?
2. Why does knowing that others are going through difficulties make us feel better?

A PARENT'S PRAYER

Heavenly Father, sometimes it seems that nobody but You knows what I am going through. Please forgive me for trying to pretend that it isn't happening to me. Lead me to people with whom I can share experiences, and as we encourage each other we can pray together. Thank You for promising that there will be no trial so bad that it will break us, but that You will give us the strength to get through it. As You make us stronger, help us to encourage others. In Jesus' name, amen.

GREAT EXPECTATIONS

"Success doesn't mean the absence of failures; it means the attainment of ultimate objectives. It means winning the war, not every battle."—Edward Bliss.

On an itinerary for Adventist Development and Relief Agency (ADRA) in Africa, I visited a young missionary mother. She told me that just prior to leaving for overseas she had attended the wedding of her younger sister. At the reception she asked, "How many children do you and Tom plan to have?"

"We don't plan to reproduce ourselves," her sister replied.

The missionary mother could hardly believe the answer.

Never mind that Scripture says: "Lo, children are an heritage of the Lord: and the fruit of the womb is his reward. As arrows are in the hand of a mighty man; so are children of the youth. Happy is the man that hath his quiver full of them" (Ps. 127:3-5). There was a time not so long ago when to get married and have a family was what life was about. Nowadays, many people regard marriage as an option and having a family as too great an expense.

In Africa I was impressed to see young women working with babies strapped to their backs. When I asked a young mother about it, she smiled and said, "Backs are for babies."

Although Scripture is not explicit on this matter, we believe that the first thing God did when He finished creating was to conduct a marriage ceremony, thereby establishing the first home. According to Genesis 4:1, Eve, the mother of us all, considered her first son a gift from the Lord.

Martin Luther translated the Hebrew in this verse to its most obvious meaning: "I have gotten a man, the Lord." He, along with many church fathers, assumed that she felt Cain was the child God had promised in Genesis 3:15. If this were indeed the case, imagine how great Eve's disappointment must have been when Cain murdered Abel and then had to leave both home and "the presence of the Lord" (4:16).

But times have changed. Today many women look upon pregnancy as something to be avoided and even terminated at will. The act of sexual intercourse, which between husband and wife was intended to demonstrate love as well as produce a family, has now become the obsession of society. Sexual activity outside marriage has become rampant, and children are in some cases actually throwaways.

Not long ago an insurance company conducted a nationwide online survey of married Americans to discover what they considered most important to them. The results indicated that 45 percent considered their cars to be the most important thing in their lives. Only 6 percent rated their children as most important, and just 10 percent said that their spouse was most important to them.

Although many couples think having children is too expensive, they often happily pay $25,000 or more for a car, which will plunge in value during the next two years and eventually end up in a junkyard. Many consider a house a more important investment than children, yet it seems to me that children are all we'll be able to take with us to heaven aside from our character.

I'm one of four children, and so is my wife. I was 19 years old when we married, and our first little girl came along 14 months later while we were at the seminary. Our goal was to have four children, and we achieved it. I really can't remember when I was not married and didn't have children!

By today's standards my wife and I were poor when we started out. For that matter, by today's standards almost everyone back then was poor. Credit cards barely existed. (The first credit card was "invented" in 1952 by the Franklin National Bank in New York, but the first nationally accepted credit cards weren't issued until 1959 in California by the Bank of America.) Most couples had only one car. An ordained minister's basic salary was $84 a week.

In those days the mothers raised the children and the fathers earned the living. I simply emulated the model I'd grown up with. Nine years after we married, we were living in Pakistan, where we had our fourth child, a boy. After working in southern Asia for a few years, we eventually moved to South America, where the children were raised in a Latin American culture.

Looking back, I believe that although I was undoubtedly negligent in some things (Matt. 23:23), more than anything else I was naive. My wife and I had established a Christian home. I was a pastor, and she and the children were always on the front row when I preached. Later, when the children got older, we even began to sing special music as a family. Our favorite was "His Banner Over Me," which we sang in Spanish.

We had family worship every night. We read *Uncle Arthur's Bedtime Stories* and *The Bible Story* series from cover to cover. We taught the children to pray. We did what one is supposed to do, and we had great expectations.

My wife was totally committed to the children. In those days we hadn't heard the terms *stress* and *burnout*, and I don't remember having used a baby-sitter very often. We were a family, and everything we did, we did together.

We returned to the States when the youngest was 7 and the oldest a teenager. Life in Washington, D.C., was not the same as in Santiago, Chile. I became deeply involved in my work with ADRA, but I wasn't worried. I had great expectations. One of these was that as soon as my children were old enough they'd find jobs. I began earning money when I was only 12, and later I worked my way through academy and college. My expectation was that my children would do the same.

I talked with my children about work. I even found jobs for them. But I don't remember talking with them about the danger of drugs or teenage pregnancy. After all, we were close as a family. The children were all in church school and academy. It never occurred to me that we were at risk, but amid my ignorance the clouds were gathering.

They say that no two children are born into the same family. Our eldest was born to parents barely in their 20s who were still in school and had no other children. The second was born into a home with one child, and where the father was a minister. The third was born into a home with parents in their mid-20s and two children. And finally the youngest was born to a missionary family on the other side of the world.

Not only does each child arrive to a different family, but also each child is definitely unique. I wish I'd been more conscious of this at the time. Raising a child is not a rubber-stamp operation. Too often we try to make each child turn out the same as the others, when in fact each one is a custom edition.

One of the children was strong-willed. On more than one occasion when we tried to discipline her, she'd be the one with the determined look on her face, and I'd be the one crying. With her it was continually a battle as to who was in charge.

One of the most difficult texts for me to wrap my mind around is the one in Proverbs 22:6, which says, "Train up a child in the way he should go: and when he is old, he will not depart from it."

I've searched here and there trying to discover what the text really means. Someone suggested that the key word in the text is "he," and that to raise up a child in the way "he" should go refers to the importance of custom-raising each child according to his or her own special needs. I think the advice that we should individualize training is cogent, but is that really what the proverb means? Others believe that the text is saying if we raise up children correctly, even though they may drift away at some point, when they get older they'll come back. But does that always happen? Does every wayward child become a returning prodigal?

Spin it however you wish, but if the guidelines for un-derstanding Scripture begin with the obvious intention of the text, then the verse seems to say that if we raise our chil-dren right, they'll turn out right. If this is indeed what it's saying, then the converse is the part that really hurts—if we don't raise our children right, they won't turn out right or worse yet, if our children haven't turned out right, guess who's to blame. But leaving the ideal for a moment, what about parents who themselves weren't Christians when they raised their families? And what about instances in which one spouse was not a Christian, and for every step the be-lieving spouse took the children forward, the other spouse led them two steps backward?

Although my wife and I had high hopes, we obviously did some things wrong and omitted others. Even though we had family worship and read *Child Guidance,* apparently that wasn't enough. As we discussed this text together, we con-cluded that when all is said and done, no matter how good we were as parents, it is God who saves our children.

Obviously this doesn't mean that we can give up and expect God to do it all. What it does say is that although we've all missed the mark ("For all have sinned, and come short of the glory of God" [Rom. 3:23]), only Jesus' blood can take away our sins as well as the sins of our children (1 John 1:7).

The text that enjoins us to raise our children in the way they should go sets a high standard. It's such a high standard that even the one who wrote it—Solomon—did not attain it. But we would have it no other way. The Christian life is not about never making mistakes, but rather about the tension between the high ideal and the reality of living in a sinful world. And as we come to grips with the meaning of it all, we don't give up hope. Instead, by faith we reach out and with the apostle Paul exclaim, "I can do all things through Christ which strengtheneth me" (Phil. 4:13).

We aren't the first parents to have great expectations. There was once a couple who lived during the time of the judges of Israel. The husband's name was Manoah. We don't know the name of his wife, but the Lord promised them a child. They were given specific prenatal instructions, and told how the child was to be raised. Verse 24 of Judges 13 says, "And the woman bare a son, and called his name Samson: and the child grew, and the Lord blessed him."

If that were all there was to the story it would be great, but the next three chapters tell of a longhaired, backslidden womanizer who was into bodybuilding, and pretty well told his parents what they had to do if they wanted to keep him happy. All those years they hadn't been able to have children, and now when God answered their prayers this was what they got—Samson!

Then there's the story of another couple who prayed for a child. God answered their prayer, and to them also was born a son. God told them to name him John. Jesus said that no one ever born was greater than John the Baptist (Matt. 11:11). I hope his aged parents weren't still alive when he was thrown into prison and soon after beheaded by order of the king.

Another couple had two boys—Jacob and Esau. One became a man of God and progenitor of Jesus. The other dropped out of sight after a few chapters, although his descendants frequently caused problems for God's people elsewhere in Scripture. Religion and eternal values seem to have meant nothing to Esau. The boys were twins, but went in opposite directions.

By now you may be thinking, *Pastor O'Ffill, you remind me of the person who was sitting alone and feeling terrible, when suddenly a voice from nowhere said, "Cheer up; things could be worse." So he cheered up, and sure enough, things got worse!*

I've heard some say that it would be better not to have children at all if this is what it's like, especially in the last days. Although there are times when rearing children turns out to be very frustrating, we were made for such a purpose. We must not forget that everyone is someone's child. Personally, I'm thankful my parents decided to have children!

As abortion increases in the U.S., so does the number of illegitimate births. Has it occurred to you that although there's illegitimate sex (sex outside of marriage), there are no illegitimate children? As soon as children are brought into this world they become persons for whom Christ died, and thus candidates for eternal life. The Bible tells us that we are not our own. We have been bought with a price (1 Cor. 6:19, 20). Our children belong to God. They are truly God's special way of helping us understand how He puts up with us.

Our family used to enjoy the hobby of raising French poodles. It's less risky to buy a poodle than to have a son or a daughter. A poodle will love you and never betray you, whereas children may one day say they don't love you, and may for a time seem to betray you. Yet I would rather be remembered as a father and a grandfather than as a breeder of poodles.

One day we got a call from a lady who had bought a poodle from us a number of years before. It had died, and now she wanted to replace it. She told me that Fifi had made a wonderful pet, and even knew how to ring a bell when she wanted to go outdoors. I figured a dog that would ring a bell to go outside is almost like a circus dog. We were happy, though, to sell her another poodle.

Some months later the woman phoned to tell us how happy she was with her new pet. She interrupted her conversation to say, "Just a minute, Gigi is ringing the bell. She wants to go outside." I thought to myself, *These are not circus dogs; this is a circus lady! She has taught these dogs to perform.*

I may not have been a circus parent, but I can't remember waking up in the morning thinking that what I wanted to do that day was to mess up my children's lives. I did the best I could at the time. The good part is that although I apparently didn't raise up my children in the way they should go, God isn't finished with them yet. And though He is graciously preparing a crown and a mansion for me, I'm telling Him, "That's OK, Lord. You can keep the mansions—please just save my children." And I still have great expectations.

CONSIDER THESE THINGS

1. No two children are born into the same family, and each child is a limited edition.
2. Even if we are perfect parents, Jesus is still the one who must save our children.

3. Although there is illegitimate sex, there are no illegitimate children in God's eyes.
4. It's less risky to raise dogs than to raise children.

DISCUSS WITH SOMEONE

1. Why does society seem to consider a sports car a better investment than a college education for a child? What philosophy lies behind such thinking?
2. What are some ways in which we can treat each member of the family as special?

A PARENT'S PRAYER

Dear heavenly Father, we are thankful that even though You knew in advance that we wouldn't do everything right, through our parents You went ahead and created us. And You didn't make us all the same. Sometimes we feel guilty when we read the text that seems to be saying if we raise our children right, they will sooner or later be OK. One thing is sure, Lord: we can't go back and raise them again! This means we have to trust in You, and because we can't see the end from the beginning as You can, this is sometimes not easy. Father, You haven't given up on us. Help us not to lose our expectations. In Jesus' name, amen.

THREE

WHY HAVE YOU DONE THIS TO ME?

"Nothing in life is so hard that you can't make it easier by the way you take it."—Ellen Glasgow.

Perhaps you've heard the expression "Get real!" Rightly understood, there's nothing more meaningful, vibrant, and real than a life in Christ; and nothing more shallow, fake, and unreal than a life without Him. I say "rightly understood" because some people believe a person comes to Jesus to get away from the painful reality of life. Nothing could be further from the truth. We come to Jesus not to escape life but to be able to survive it.

On one occasion Jesus offered, "Come unto me, all ye that labour and are heavy laden, and I will give you rest. Take my yoke upon you, and learn of me; for I am meek and lowly in heart: and ye shall find rest unto your souls. For my yoke is easy, and my burden is light" (Matt. 11:28-30).

Some could interpret these words to mean that when we come to Jesus our burdens go away or become lighter. Though we could wish it were that way, it isn't so. In Bible times people carried burdens by hanging them from a yoke that fit across their shoulders. Being a carpenter by trade, Jesus probably made many such yokes. He recognized a good one from a bad one, and He knew that if a yoke didn't fit on the neck just right, it could make the load impossible to carry for very long.

The burden we all carry from birth to death is life itself. Jesus invites us to come to Him not to get rid of our burdens of life but to learn how to carry them. Jesus' life was one of great burdens, and even if you haven't discovered it yet, your life and mine will be the same. Although He has told us through the prophets that one day He will wipe away the tears from our eyes, that day has not yet come. And until then, tears are a part of our lives. Jesus told us what to expect: "These things I have spoken unto you, that in me ye might have peace. *In the world ye shall have tribulation:* but be of good cheer; I have overcome the world" (John 16:33).

While this book espouses the ideal and looks forward to the time when all things will be made new, it's also about reality—the here and now. It's too late for us to pray that what has happened to our families will not happen. It's already happened. The challenge we now face as parents and grandparents is what we're going to do about it, and what God can help us do to mitigate the damages.

When a child has wandered away from the Lord and is doing crazy, heart-wrenching things, it's not unusual to think (even if you never actually ask the child), *Why have you done this to me?* Although the sins of the fathers, which we will discuss in chapter 8, are visited on the children, the added tragedy of this time in history is that the sins of the children are being visited upon the parents. It isn't uncommon for grown children to bring home their own children for their parents to raise. We had this experience, raising a granddaughter for five years. I'll share more about that later.

Although we love our children, our disappointment and frustration often find expression in anger. This anger may not be mere anger of the moment, such as when we lose our temper, but a deepening, continuing anger over time.

I used to believe that I didn't have a temper. Through the

years I've discovered that I do. Though it has a long fuse and doesn't manifest itself through swearing and throwing things, it *does* damage relationships nonetheless. In my case anger comes from frustration, disappointment, or as a reaction to not feeling I'm in control of a particular situation. I don't fly off the handle, but I can tell when I'm angry, because I begin to feel it in my stomach. I express anger not so much by what I do as by what I say.

Sometimes when we speak of anger, we defend it by calling it righteous indignation. Other times we may point to Ephesians 4:26, which admonishes us to be angry and sin not. We also refer to the times Jesus became angry and, for example, proceeded to throw the money changers out of the Temple. Having righteous indignation and being angry without sinning may work for some people, but I've discovered that when I get angry, I usually end up sinning. And when I'm angry it's hard for me to be righteous!

I've also noticed that when I'm angry what I have to say at the time is usually not constructive and thus not worth saying. We often put up with a problem until we get upset and then try to solve it while we're angry. It's unfortunate that we don't address our problems *before* our tempers rise, but when we aren't angry, we don't want to talk about them!

You've probably heard the expression "Strike while the iron is hot." But in family situations experience has taught me that when the iron is hot is precisely *not* the time to strike. I'm not an expert in ferrous metals, but I understand that if you want to make a permanent change in the metal, you first get it red-hot. When it's pliable from the heat, the changes that are made are permanent.

I wish I had recognized this when the children were still young. Let me illustrate. Suppose our then teenage son is driving the car on a family outing. When he veers too close to another car, I get upset and shout, "What are you trying to do, get us all killed?"

The iron is hot. He's caught in the act. Embarrassed, his ears turn red and he mutters, "How come you're always hollering at me? Do you think I did it on purpose?"

Let's revisit this scenario. What would happen if at the time I said nothing, but later while we're working around the house I say, "I'm thankful the angels protected us this morning?"

What do you think my son would say in this case? Although we don't know for sure, he might have said something like "So am I. I didn't see the guy coming. I guess a person has to be on the lookout all the time."

You get the point. Our reactions to what our children and even our spouses do can make the situation better or worse. Anger—in my case, at least—always makes matters worse. I have come to a kind of agreement with myself. When I feel anger welling up, I disqualify myself because my anger creates a conflict of interest in whatever the problem is. I believe that even though I may have been right in the beginning, when I'm angry I've lost the moral high ground.

I try to make it a point to ask for forgiveness when I become angry. On occasion I've asked my wife for forgiveness, and she's responded, "For what?" Even though she may not have been aware I had a problem, I'm teaching myself a lesson. In my portfolio of possible reactions to a situation I do not accept anger as an option.

Some people feel that to repress anger can, in the long run, cause more damage than to let it out. In my case I don't repress my anger. I've discovered that prayer has the same effect on anger as water on a blaze. It puts it out. So when I feel anger well up, I don't repress it; I put it out with prayer.

The rebellion in heaven was against God Himself, yet instead of lashing out in anger, He reacted to save His children.

The challenge we face as parents and grandparents is that we must not consider ourselves victims. Although we may have a hundred reasons to be angry, if we're to cooperate with God for the salvation of our children, we must remind ourselves: "Let all bitterness, and wrath, and anger, and clamour, and evil speaking, be put away from you, with all malice" (Eph. 4:31).

Times come when parents feel they're being taken advantage of and wish they could say no, but feel obligated to say yes. Sometimes we may want to express how we really feel, but it would only make matters worse. How thankful I am for the biblical observation: "The love of Christ constraineth us" (2 Cor. 5:14).

The nice thing about having pets is that they seem to give more than they take. In the case of children sometimes it can, in the short run, appear to be just the opposite. One of our problems is that we've never passed this way before. Although we may have studied the subject of parenting and even may have taught seminars in family life, it doesn't make it any easier when we're told that a son or daughter has decided not to spend money to put their child in church school. We then realize that if the child is going to get a Christian education it will be up to us.

Sometimes we want to say, "Why are you doing this to *me?* I did everything I could for *you.*" Many times I need to remind myself: "When I was a child, I spake as a child, I understood as a child, I thought as a child: but when I became a man, I put away childish things" (1 Cor. 13:11).

Childhood is about being self-centered. But being adults means we've gotten past self-centeredness and are learning how to think of others rather than ourselves. This is difficult, because society actually encourages selfishness. We're urged to look out for ourselves first and not let anyone walk on us, not even our children.

You may be wondering why we should be talking about the possibility that we're angry with our children. After all, isn't our prayer "God, keep Your mansions"? I've come to the conclusion that it's in praying from the heart for my children that God is saving me. Inasmuch as God used us to create our children, if He is going to answer our prayers to save our children, He is going to need to be able to use us along the way.

We may realistically expect that our children, whether young or old, will tend to interpret who God is through us. It's my prayer that God, by His Spirit, will be able to bring the full force of conviction into my children's lives. But it's possible that my bad attitudes could keep this from happening.

We prayed for 10 years that God would restore our son. For a long time things didn't get better. At times they actually got worse. Many times we asked ourselves what good prayer did.

How often I wished that I would wake up one day and the problem would be over. The apostle Paul had what was apparently a physical problem. Some believe he had problems with his eyes, which may have been caused by his vision of Jesus on the road to Damascus. Whatever the problem, he prayed that he would be healed. Here was a man whose prayers healed others, yet they didn't seem to be working for him.

As a minister I have prayed for others, and many prayers have been answered. Nevertheless, often my prayers for my own suffering don't seem to bring results. I've found comfort in the words of Jesus to the apostle Paul, which are, I'm sure, His words to us as parents: "My grace is sufficient for thee: for my strength is made perfect in weakness. Most gladly therefore will I rather glory in my infirmities, that the power of Christ may rest upon me" (2 Cor. 12:9).

Not all problems in my family are over. The alcoholism

and drug addiction may be a thing of the past, but now unbelieving spouses and the pain of broken homes, with the impact of divorce on all of us, are the challenge and concern. It seems to be taking a long time for God to save our children, but there can be no doubt that along the way He is saving us.

Some years ago I had a bout with adhesive capsulitis (frozen shoulder). It was in my left shoulder, and without realizing it at first, I lost most of the range of motion in that arm. The treatment was physical therapy, which they sometimes refer to as PT. For me it was just that, pain and torture!

One morning I was at the clinic, and the therapist, who had a wonderful sense of humor, was giving me a treatment. I discovered that if I raised my right leg just a little bit, it affected the center of gravity, and the treatment didn't hurt so badly. Though it made the treatment less painful, it also made it less effective.

The therapist caught me in the act, and I'll never forget what she said: "You must submit. If you don't, the therapy will take longer."

The pain of the treatments was so bad that I wanted to get off the table and run away. But fortunately I wanted to get well even more. If we can trust in God and overcome the temptation to give up or to resist, He who has begun a good work in us will at last finish it (Phil. 1:6). Until then our strength is in our weakness, because it's when we're weak in our own strength that we become strong in Him.

CONSIDER THESE THINGS

1. From birth to death, life is the burden we must all carry. Those who follow Jesus carry it best.
2. Anger is often a result of our disappointment with our children.

3. When we strike when the iron is hot, it may leave permanent results that we don't want.
4. Prayer extinguishes anger.
5. When we feel weak and helpless, we are more inclined to depend on Jesus than when everything is going well.

DISCUSS WITH SOMEONE

1. Discuss how our anger may express itself in our relationship with our grown children who are disappointing us.
2. Share some experiences you have had that caused your relationship with the Lord to grow.

A PARENT'S PRAYER

Dear Father in heaven, it is hard to admit that our disappointment with our children often makes us very angry. Sometimes we wonder why they are doing this to us after all that we have tried to do for them. Lord, sometimes we do and say things that seem to make matters worse. Please forgive us. We want so much for our children to be saved! When we are tempted to have a bad attitude, may the Holy Spirit speak to us, reminding us to continue to trust You no matter how things might appear at the moment. Amen.

Four

Don't Take It Personally

"There are two ways of meeting difficulties. You alter the difficulties or you alter yourself to meet them."—Phyllis Bottome.

One day when my wife came home from work we exchanged hellos, and I continued with what I was doing. Soon I noticed that Betty's face was expressionless. At first I thought it was just a passing thing, but as the evening wore on I could see that something was definitely wrong.

After a while I said to her, "Honey, what's wrong? Did something happen at the office?"

She replied that someone had stopped by her desk, and as they had chatted, the person said, "Betty, we heard what you're going through. I want you to know I'm praying for you."

I responded, "But sweetheart, what was wrong with that?"

"Dick, I feel so guilty and ashamed! I feel I ought to wear dark glasses when I go to work. I'm beginning to understand how Mrs. Judas must have felt."

You see, our son's 15-year-old girlfriend was pregnant. He'd dropped out of college, and now we wondered what would become of the child.

Through the years people have asked me if I feel responsible for what my children have gone through. It's easy to suggest that if I'd done this or if I'd done that things would have been different. Are we to blame for what our grown children do?

To make matters worse, there may be times when an adult child has, as it were, pointed an accusing finger at the parent and said, "You never did this or that for me," or "You made me do that." As parents we need to settle this matter. Are we to blame? Should we take personal responsibility for what our own children do?

Common attitudes in contemporary society have complicated this question. Blame for so much of society's ills is placed at the feet of the parents. I can't remember another time when children publicly confessed the sins of their fathers and mothers as they do now. The message is that what they are, their parents have made them to be. Although there can be no doubt that we brought our children into the world and raised them, are we, in fact, responsible for what they presently are? Society seems to say yes.

Our apparent personal guilt has now become our corporate guilt. In studies done in recent years the data seem to indicate that in the past we were too strict with our children. Some even point out that if we hadn't been so legalistic, our children would still be in the church.

Although there is surely such a thing as legalism, I don't believe that the fact that I took my children to Sabbath school and church or that we had family worship in the home and held certain Christian standards should be classified as legalism. People who want to do God's will are not necessarily legalists. That which constitutes legalism is motivation, not activity. It seems to me that legalists are those who want to do the will of God *in their own strength or because they feel that such a lifestyle brings them merit or earns them salvation.*

We didn't force religion on our children. Of course, Betty and I maintained a Christian home before the children were born. We tried to have one when they were with us, and now that they're grown we continue to uphold the same standards we've always held dear.

If I could be criticized for something, it might be that I felt I owed it to the Lord to maintain an ambience in the home that would honor Him. I can remember telling the children when they reached their teens that inasmuch as anywhere they might live would probably have house rules, we were going to insist they be home by midnight on weekends and 11:00 p.m. during the week. And I don't believe we were wrong in setting such curfews.

Some might not agree with us, but we never made a big deal about music. We simply told the children that if they wanted to listen to their own special music, they could do so with earphones on. Playing music without earphones is like smoking. When one person smokes, everyone smokes!

Having rules and regulations in the home is not legalism, or necessarily the reason young people leave the church. A few years ago an entertainer popularized the saying "The devil made me do it." Now the retort seems to be "My parents [or the church] made me do it." No, I don't think the problem lies with the rules.

Looking back, I recall times when my attitude wasn't what it ought to have been. Rather than change the rules, perhaps we parents need to change our attitudes, and thankfully God can help us with that. But before we put on dark glasses and consider ourselves total failures, we must factor in the role played by society as a whole. Once upon a time the home, the church, and the school—in that order—made the greatest impact on children. Those three influences have now been overtaken by the impact of peer pressure, which has resulted in *peer dependency.*

Peer pressure is a given, like barometric pressure. Our children do not go wrong because of peer pressure but because of peer dependency. Peer dependency is looking to others—friends, television, movies, music, or magazines—for cues about what is acceptable or not acceptable for one's own life, and being motivated by a desire to accommodate these external influences. Peer dependency is not a phenomenon that ends after the teenage years. It can become a motivating force even in an adult's life.

The apostle Paul asks, "Know ye not, that to whom ye yield yourselves servants to obey, his servants ye are to whom ye obey; whether of sin unto death, or of obedience unto righteousness?" (Rom. 6:16).

Lately my son and I have had several conversations about his prodigal years. On more than one occasion he's told me, "Dad, it wasn't your fault. I was selfish and interested in pleasing no one but myself." I appreciate his candidness. This model fits the teaching of Scripture that says: "For we must all appear before the judgment seat of Christ; that every one may receive the things done in his body, according to that he hath done, whether it be good or bad" (2 Cor. 5:10).

This text is clear. It teaches that not just the parents will be judged, but that all of us must give account for how we have lived. This includes one's children. We are all responsible for what we do. When I preach on this subject I often point out that although we didn't get to choose our parents or the way we were brought up, we definitely get to choose how we're going to live today.

One day two friends were talking. One was telling the other about something he'd done that he later regretted. "But," he explained, "I had to do it."

"Was there anything else you could have done instead?" asked his friend.

Not answering the question, the other replied, "But I *had* to do it."

"Were there any other options?" his friend insisted.

"Yes, I suppose there were."

"Then you didn't *have* to do it," continued his friend.

"No, I guess I didn't" was the reply.

Inasmuch as life is made up of choices, each of us must accept responsibility for our own actions. I'm responsible for the way I behaved as a father, and my grown children are responsible for what they're doing now.

As long as we continue to rationalize either our own behavior or theirs, we will not be able to get past our mistakes. To say "The reason I did that was . . ." can imply that should the same circumstances arise again, I would probably do the same thing again. An old adage says, "Live and learn." I wish that were true. Unfortunately, for many it's "Live and never learn."

By holding us responsible for what we do, God does us a great favor. To do anything short of that would be to consider us lesser life forms. No one condemns a snake for striking.

Understanding that we must not take personally what our children are doing doesn't mean we're trying to shift the perception of blame from ourselves to them. The issue isn't who's to blame, but who's accountable. Our children are accountable for the lives they now live. There are options. They, like us, have choices.

If we're going to help a floundering swimmer, we must have our own heads above water. Likewise, if we're to help our children, we need, by God's power, to be emotionally and spiritually healthy. We must be free from anger, shame, and guilt. We must be free in order to help God set them free.

A mother was sharing with me her concern for her children. With tears in her voice she recounted that through the years she and her husband had always put their children first. Concern for the children had impacted where they had lived and even the work they had chosen to do. They wanted to make sure everything they did would have a positive impact on their children.

Now the children were grown, and their interest in spiritual things had diminished. Often they didn't go to church, and the Sabbath didn't have the meaning it once had. The mother's disappointment was understandable.

In contrast, I know of a couple in which the wife was raised a member of the church. But she gave it up when she married, and they raised three children with little or no religious training. When the children reached their teens, lo and behold, they became interested in spiritual things and made a commitment to the Lord!

These anomalies are difficult, if not impossible, to explain.

But as parents, and later as grandparents, we must move on. Our children are not babies anymore, and we must not be babies either. Jesus has a work to do in our hearts, just as we are praying He will work in the hearts of our children. How can we pray that our children will be changed if we continue to hold on to guilt, bitterness, and even anger?

When I was 18, I caught my arm in a cement mixer. Someone told me that at the point of the break, the bones would knit and actually be stronger than the rest of the arm. I don't know if this is true, but I like the idea. At the very point where we are broken and healed in the experiences of our lives, we can actually become stronger. I love the promise "He healeth the broken in heart, and bindeth up their wounds" (Ps. 147:3).

CONSIDER THESE THINGS

1. Having rules in the home should not be confused with legalism.
2. Peer dependency can continue after the teen years.

3. In making choices there is always more than one option.
4. Sometimes children will choose to serve the Lord even though they have not received encouragement from their parents. The opposite is also true.
5. Jesus needs to work in our hearts as much as He needs to work in the hearts of our children.

DISCUSS WITH SOMEONE

1. Why must we accept responsibility for our actions?
2. Discuss the differences between peer pressure and peer dependency.

A PARENT'S PRAYER

Dear God, sometimes we feel we are responsible for the way our children have turned out. We tried to raise them to love and respect You, and now some are saying that we were legalists. Lord, we thought we were doing the right things.

Help us realize that our children are now on their own, and able to make their own decisions. Please work in our hearts so that we can know how we can best help them. In Jesus' name, amen.

I Don't Want to Look Anymore

"Only those who do nothing make no mistakes."
—Anonymous.

We were walking together through a village in Pakistan. My companion was the president of a local mission. I was in my early 30s; he was in his 50s. As we walked down a dusty path bordered with mud houses on both sides, he commented, "I can't think of anything heaven would have that you don't already have in the United States."

Through the years I've pondered what he said that hot afternoon in the Punjab. Of course eyes have not seen and ears have not heard the things God has prepared for those who love Him (Isa. 64:4; 1 Cor. 2:9). Nevertheless, during the past 50 years there has been a mad rush, as it were, to create heaven here on earth, at least as far as material things are concerned.

Fifty years ago Adventists preached a lot of sermons about the soon coming of Jesus. Inasmuch as He still hasn't come, some find it embarrassing to continue to preach about it. Besides, when you have two cars, a new house, and a nice young family, there isn't the sense of urgency there might have been during one of the world wars or when times were hard.

My early life was sheltered. Our family enjoyed wonderful health as I was growing up, and even as Betty and I raised our children, they were rarely sick, for which we were thankful. Our extended family on both sides were members of the Adventist Church. I never knew my grandfathers, but I loved my grandmothers, even though I saw them only once a year. When they passed away I missed them, but it was not a shock, because in my mind I can't remember when they weren't old.

With my parents it's a different matter. I can remember when they were young. My mother had black hair and blue eyes. My father was tall and good-looking. My memories of home are all positive. I was in the seminary when their first grandchild was born. We took the baby to visit them in Ohio. They were delighted that Betty and I were doing well and had made them grandparents.

During our years of service in the mission field we kept in touch the best we could. When we finally returned to the States, my parents lived only 100 miles away, so we saw them several times a month. Then we moved to Florida, so we didn't get to see them as often. While we were passing through the difficult years with the children, my parents remained supportive and always remarked how much they loved their grandchildren and then their great grandchildren. But old age moved in. We began to notice the changes. They were not only becoming old; they were also beginning to look old and act old.

I can't remember when my grandparents weren't old. It sounds ridiculous, I know, but I must have figured they had always been old! But it came as a shock to watch my parents age. Mother passed away, and later Dad had two strokes, becoming very frail. Gone is the handsome, enthusiastic minister who'd been such a role model for me.

As all this was happening, I began to realize that even a newborn baby is born OAP—old age positive—even though no symptoms show up until the person reaches about 45 years of age. As I saw the ravages of old age wreak havoc on my parents, I realized that I, too, will grow old. Someone has said that 40 is the old age of youth and 50 is the youth of old age. With exception of Enoch and Elijah, the mortality rate for the human race is 100 percent, just in case you haven't noticed.

The time comes when it can appear as though life is crumbling on both ends. Has it happened to you that while the grown children seem to be taking less and less interest in spiritual things and their lives in some cases are coming apart, at the other end of the spectrum those who took care of us when we were babies are becoming totally dependent on us, either physically or emotionally?

There were the good years when these kinds of things were happening to everyone else but us, so we didn't have to notice. In my ministry countless times I've visited the sick in the hospital, but it's a different story when the person lying in the bed and asking for a urinal is your own father. Needless to say, it has its impact.

I know a man who retired at age 40 and then worked for years with the refugees in Southeast Asia as a volunteer. He woke up one morning after being married for 35 years and heard his wife, whom he loved very much, declare the marriage over—she wanted out.

He assured me that he still believed God had a plan for him. I asked him if that plan included his wife's leaving him. I wasn't trying to be facetious. It is important that we get a handle on this, because if we don't, it is easy to come to the same conclusion as the Muslims: everything that happens is the will of God.

Although God has a plan for everyone born into the world, how thankful I am that He also has any number of contingency plans. The good news is that we can never get ourselves into a corner so tight that God doesn't have a way for us to get on with our journey to heaven. Although all roads don't lead to heaven, Jesus is willing to lead us there from wherever we may find ourselves, wherever He finds us.

We often hear that God is in control. Although it's safe to say He is in control of the ship in which we are riding, it's important to remember that He is not sponsoring all that is going on aboard the ship!

I've finally come to realize that life isn't about living in a nice house or owning two cars and a boat. Life is about families—children, grandchildren, and, yes, about the incurable disease of old age. Old age was always there, but I didn't have to look. Now it's in my face, and I have no place to hide.

Human nature doesn't like to face unpleasant truth. We want to get away from it. We're accustomed to having someone else or something else do the dirty work. I like to joke that our lives are so mechanized that we can be doing the laundry, washing the dishes, mixing up a loaf of bread, listening to the radio, and mowing the lawn all at the same time!

When we get a headache or an upset stomach, there's usually something in the medicine cabinet to take away the pain. If you can't sleep at night, the doctor will give you something to help. We can pay to have someone take care of the children and can find a place for our parents to spend their last years, but what pill do we take for a heavy or broken heart?

When we look at things the way they sometimes are, it reminds me of what someone said with tongue in cheek: "We have come to a fork in the road. One road leads to hopelessness and despair, and the other to oblivion. I only hope we have the wisdom to take the right road!"

Question: What are we supposed to do when sometimes it seems as though things are closing in on every side? So much of our lives has to do with our expectations. Answer: When life doesn't meet our expectations, we may have to lower our expectations. Many have the idea that only good things happen to the good guys, and that bad things happen only to the bad guys. This kind of thinking makes it difficult to face reality and see things the way they really are. When we truly comprehend the reality of this life, two things will happen. First, we'll stop trying to create heaven here on earth. Second, we'll begin to get serious about the coming of Jesus. It's one thing to be under the illusion that young people are going to stay young, but it's quite another thing to realize that, barring the coming of Jesus, this life in and of itself is literally a dead end.

I've noticed that as long as I feel I'm in control, I don't need Jesus very much. But comes the day when I see things the way they really are, and suddenly I'm aware that without Jesus this life is going nowhere. Lord Belhaven must have realized this long ago when he quoted John Flavel to the Scottish Parliament in 1706: "Man's extremity is God's opportunity."

The children of Israel were fleeing Egypt and soon found themselves with mountains on each side, an army behind them, and a sea in front. This was God's opportunity. When we encounter some of life's most difficult situations, that is when God can do the most for us.

Often we're God's foul-weather friends. We don't think we need Him when life's sun is shining. I'm glad God isn't like us. If we treated our friends the way we, who say we are God's friends, treat Him, soon we wouldn't have any friends.

In case you came from another planet, let me tell you what it's like to live here. "In the world ye shall have tribulation" (John 16:33). "Yet man is born unto trouble, as the sparks fly upward" (Job 5:7). Sometimes I say to people, "In my life I've had trouble." Then I ask, "Have you had any trouble . . . yet?" They'll inevitably smile.

But even knowing that this is the way things are in life, it still gets pretty tiresome just hanging on. Sometimes I wish it would all go away so that I could get on with my life. I've discovered that the burdens of life don't get lighter with the passing years—they get heavier. But that seems to be what it takes for this know-it-all generation to run up the white flag and shout like Peter when he started going down for the third time, "Lord, save me" (Matt. 14:30).

"Heal me, O Lord, and I shall be healed; save me, and I shall be saved: for thou art my praise" (Jer. 17:14).

I can finally say, "It's OK. We can look now." You mean, Pastor O'Ffill, your problems are gone? No, they are still there. But we can look now. By now you may be thinking that this chapter has made your problems worse. First, you were concerned about your children, and now you've been reminded of your parents'—and even of your own—mortality.

I haven't told you something you didn't already know. Maybe you too haven't wanted to look anymore, or have been trying to forget. Although we know what reality is and that we must live in reality, we must not put our hope in what we can do, or in a heaven we may have tried to create here on earth. This world is not our home; we're just a-passin' through. Remember?

Jesus invites us to take up our cross and follow Him. Though we pray to Him with our heads down and our eyes closed, we cannot meet the challenges of life with our eyes closed, but must do so with our eyes wide open and our heads up.

The weight of an object is measured in terms of the strength necessary to move it. For me 50 pounds isn't heavy, but 150 pounds is. We must all bear the weight of life. It would be a mistake to think that our lives all weigh the same. Some have tremendous burdens to carry.

We often must remind ourselves of the text that gives us hope and makes it possible to keep moving with our heads up and our eyes wide open: "There hath no temptation taken you but such as is common to man: but God is faithful, who will not suffer you to be tempted above that ye are able; but will with the temptation also make a way to escape, that ye may be able to bear it" (1 Cor. 10:13).

The meaning is obvious. On occasion I've seen people with severe disabilities and thought to myself, *I don't have the strength to bear that kind of burden.* The truth is I don't—I don't because I'm not there. But if I were—or if I should ever be—I have the comfort of the promise that He will at that time give me the strength necessary to carry the load. His own load was neither easy nor light, except through the strength that His Father gave Him to carry it. I take comfort from that. Betty and I are discovering that despite the additional burden of aged parents piled atop the burden of children and grandchildren, His grace is sufficient. Through His help I'm not afraid to look anymore.

CONSIDER THESE THINGS

1. No matter how close we are to God, we can expect that this life will be full of trouble.
2. You can't make a silk purse out of a sow's ear. Don't try to create heaven here on earth.
3. God takes us where He finds us, and we can never get so lost that He can't find us.
4. Not looking at problems doesn't make them go away. Ignorance is not necessarily bliss.
5. God's grace is sufficient, one day at a time.

DISCUSS WITH SOMEONE

1. What can we do to prepare for old age?
2. Someone has said that how much something weighs depends on the pull of the earth. What significance does this have in respect to the Christian's life?

A PRAYER FOR THE AGED

Holy Father, we want to take a special minute to pray for the aged. Lord, we recognize that the wages of sin is death for all of us, and our hearts go out at this time to remember those who are even now passing through the valley of the shadow. Please comfort the aged. So many of them have believed that Jesus would return while they were young, and now they may feel disappointed and perhaps even wonder if You still care. Please be with them.

Help us prepare for our own old age by being sympathetic and kind. Give us a spirit of compassion so that we may think not of what we can do to make ourselves happy, but rather what we can do each day to encourage and help others, especially the aged. Teach us what it means to bind up the brokenhearted and comfort those who mourn.

We look forward to the day when our parents and grandparents will be clothed with eternal youth and when You will at last wipe away all tears from our eyes. We give praise to Him who is the resurrection and the life. Amen.

Six

ACCEPTING THE UNACCEPTABLE

"Acceptance of what has happened is the first step to overcoming the consequence of any misfortune."—William James.

It has been said that if men had to go through pregnancy, there wouldn't be many children. My wife's pregnancies weren't complicated, only super miserable. The first one was bad; the second, worse. At one point she had go to the hospital because she hadn't been able to eat or drink, so her electrolytes went out of balance. We were glad when the third pregnancy went a little better. The fourth was the best, probably because in Pakistan, where we were at the time, there was someone else to do the cooking.

It's not unusual for a woman to go through pregnancy vowing she'll not do it again. But when the baby arrives, she changes her mind and decides that really it would be best for the child to have a brother or sister.

When an unpleasant experience is finite, that is, has a beginning and a predictable end, we will often "bite the bullet" and pay the price for the reward we know we'll get down the line. But when our children seem to have left the Lord, there's no guarantee they'll ever return. If only we could know that their wandering is for a year or two or even 10, at least we could do an emotional countdown.

Because we often cannot see a future resolution, we experience a sense of dread and hopelessness. One morning very early I saw a light under the door of my son's room. Anxious to know if he were in some sort of trouble, I went outside the house, where in the darkness I could look in through the window.

He was on his bed, propped up on his elbows. He had earphones on and seemed to be looking at a book. For an instant hope flashed, and I wondered if maybe he were having morning devotions. Then I saw him flick a lighter. He held something in his mouth. He was, as they say, doing crack. (Fortunately the Lord spared him from becoming addicted to this drug.)

For a split second—though I am ashamed to say it now—I thought it would be better if he were dead. At least if he were dead, he wouldn't be heading into a living death, and I wouldn't have to watch the terrible process. But the dead can't change. I needed to be reminded right then that where there's life there's hope. Although I could not know it at the time, my son would be healed. Alas, it would take 10 years.

I cannot say what it is like to have a child who is physically disabled. I do know what it's like to have a child who is spiritually disabled. Sometimes I wonder if it's easier to accept the former than the latter. In the case of a disabled child, we don't blame them. In the case of the latter, what they're doing seems to be on purpose, and this greatly changes the equation.

One day my son and I were sitting in an Italian restaurant. I don't remember how the matter came up or what we were talking about at the time, but my son asked, "Dad, why don't you just accept me the way I am?" He'd turned his back on all the things his mother and I had tried to do for him through the years, and I understood him to be saying, "Why not just give up trying to change me? I am the way I am." But how could I do that? Accept him the way he was? He had to be kidding!

Looking back now, I can see that it is indeed possible for a parent to accept a child without accepting the unacceptable. To be able to do this a person has to give up trying to change the other person. But this isn't easy. Training a child is changing a child, and you do not stop doing that from one day to the next. Give up hoping my son would change? Never! But if he was going to change, I had to change the way I was relating to him.

It's easy for our lives to become completely taken over by loved ones. Their good days become our good days, and their bad days become our bad days. Some young people like to ride on roller coasters. Roller coasters make me nauseated. Often our children's lives become like a roller coaster.

We parents must somehow get off the roller coaster. In the world of the families of addicts they call this process detachment. At first glance parents who love their wayward child might think that love demands more attachment, not less. The word "detach" has several meanings, including "remove from association with," "divorce," "sever," or "disjoin." However, other meanings include "disengage," "disconnect," and "uncouple."

When we pray for our children, it's important to remember that God died not only to save our loved one but also to save us. Although we pray that we might be saved as families, only the Holy Spirit can accomplish this—one at a time, and He can begin with us.

We can know that we need to detach from our children if our faith in God soars when they're up and plummets when they're down. One day my son and I were painting a bedroom. He told me he had decided to live right. Tears of joy coursed down my cheeks. I wouldn't learn until later that there come times when a person will try to manipulate others by telling them what they want to hear. This isn't uncommon and, as you may have experienced, can cause emotional and spiritual whiplash to the parent or the spouse who cares so much.

The inability to detach can result not only in a roller-coaster relationship with God but also in alienation of those relationships that are nearest and dearest to us. Through the years I've applied and recommended to others the principles of detachment.

In detachment we learn:

1. Not to suffer because of the actions or reactions of other people.
2. Not to allow ourselves to be used or abused by others in the interest of making them better.
3. Not to do for others what they could do for themselves.
4. Not to cover up for anyone's mistakes or misdeeds.
5. Not to prevent a crisis if it is in the natural course of events.

In the context of wayward children we have much to learn from this list:

1. Of course we will suffer, but we must not lose our faith in God.
2. We must be alert to instances in which our loved ones try to exploit our love. If they succeed, this will tend to encourage the rebellion.
3. Although we will do for them what we can, we must not try to do for them what only they can do for themselves.
4. Although we want to be there when they need us, we are not there to cover up or hide the wrong that they're doing.
5. We'll remember the text that says we reap what we sow (Gal. 6:7). Our loved ones will continue going in the direction they're headed until they themselves can't

stand it any longer. During the time the prodigal son had money and girlfriends, he wasn't thinking of going home. It was only when he felt like a pig that he decided he'd had enough.

One day a mother approached me at church. She had a prayer request. "My son isn't a believer. He's out of work. Please pray that he'll find work." Thinking about this later, I decided it would have been better had she said, "My son isn't a believer. He's out of work. Please pray that this crisis will bring him back to the Lord."

It's easy to fall into the habit of praying, "God, bless our children." To pray "God, save our children" is quite another thing. It's usually necessary that sin be allowed to follow its natural course, and God does not often step in to interfere with the law of cause and effect. He is there, however, at every step of the way and is very willing to mitigate damages. But human nature being what it is, God often isn't called until it's time to pick up the pieces.

Coming to Jesus is always about brokenness. "The sacrifices of God are a broken spirit: a broken and a contrite heart, O God, thou wilt not despise" (Ps. 51:17). People cannot make genuine changes in their lives with heads held high, "for God resisteth the proud, and giveth grace to the humble" (1 Peter 5:5). Another text says: "Humble yourselves in the sight of the Lord, and he shall lift you up" (James 4:10).

Our children won't return to the God of their parents until circumstances in their life are such that they cannot bear it anymore. We must be prepared to see this happen.

Sometimes I think it's easier to suffer ourselves than to see those we love suffer. When we suffer, we can do something about it, but when our loved ones suffer, we feel helpless. Every parent can remember taking a little one to the doctor for some reason or another and standing by helplessly while the child screamed and cried. Afterward we took the youngster into our arms, and how tightly he or she clung to us. And we told them how much we loved them as we wiped the tears from their little eyes.

It's different yet it's the same when years later the children, who now have children of their own, are getting a divorce, and things are going on that they don't want to talk about. They may tell you that when they go home at night they curl up and cry until they can hardly stop. We would like to take them into our arms again and hold them close. We have a pretty good idea what's going on, but they don't want to talk about it, so we watch them cry, and we cry too. The situation is unacceptable. Yes, we know that we must accept it for now, but we won't accept it forever. We will pray, "Lord, thanks, but You can keep Your mansions; You can keep Your crowns; just save our children."

And so, son, to answer your question "Why don't you accept me the way I am?" I reply, "I'll never be satisfied with the way you are now. I won't be happy until you have given your heart back to Jesus." I have tears in my eyes as I speak. Then I notice he has tears in his eyes too.

CONSIDER THESE THINGS

1. Where there is life there is hope.
2. Some children are physically disabled. Others are, for the time being, spiritually disabled.
3. We can accept our children as individuals without accepting their sinful behaviors.
4. We must not allow our adult children to set the agenda for our lives.
5. Being emotionally detached from our children doesn't mean we don't love them.

DISCUSS WITH SOMEONE

1. Discuss what detachment would look like in your own life.
2. How is it possible to be too helpful to our children?

A GRANDPARENT'S PRAYER

Dear God, when we thought of having children, it never occurred to us that one day we would have grandchildren. What a joy they are to us! We are so thankful that You have enriched our lives through them. Yet, Lord, when there is divorce and unhappiness, it breaks our hearts. Our grandchildren are so innocent. They didn't ask to be born into a broken home. Please have the angels be especially close to them. Protect them from evil on the outside and from the influence of evil that the devil may bring to them as temptation.

We love them in a different way than we love even our own children. Please give them special grace to keep them from becoming discouraged. Help us know how to love them so that in times of insecurity they may feel secure in our love for them. Lord, we are praying that You will save them and their parents. In Jesus' name, amen.

SEVEN

IF YOU REALLY LOVED ME

"Experience is what you get when you do not get what you want."—Anonymous.

The sign on the desk said, "I didn't know when the plot thickened I would be in the middle of it." Many times I think back to the time when my intended and I stood facing my minister father. We were in the Kress Memorial church in Winter Park, Florida, and the customary question was asked: "Do you promise to love, honor, and cherish, in sickness and in health, in prosperity and in adversity, for better or for worse, till death do you part?"

Of course, we both said we would, but like most young people, at the time we didn't have a clue!

At a church potluck I once watched a man patiently feeding his wife. It was obvious from the expression on her face she had Alzheimer's disease. I thought of our vows: "in sickness and in health." Another time I met a man wheeling his wife through the supermarket. I commented to him about the wedding vows and how, at the time, we had no idea it was going to be like this. His smile let me know he understood.

If we knew what was going to happen to us on a day-by-day basis, we'd probably be afraid to get out of bed in the morning. Fear and worry can literally make it difficult to function. How thankful I am that the trouble sin has caused didn't make God dysfunctional.

He has always been who He is. He was forgiving before there was anyone to forgive. Often people wonder why, if He knew all this was going to happen, He proceeded with Creation. If He hadn't proceeded, it would have meant He was weak and fearful. When this sad chapter in the history of the universe is closed, Murphy's Law, which says that if something can go wrong, it will, will be annulled. God promised His ancient people: "Affliction shall not rise up the second time" (Nahum 1:9).

When children have trouble, it can adversely affect the parents' marriage. It should not be surprising that each parent may deal with grief in a different way. It's been my experience that the father will tend to take a hard line, whereas the mother will be more forgiving. Yet it can easily be the other way around.

I was introduced to a couple who had recently learned that one of their sons had multiple sclerosis. On the one hand, the father, a physician, was eager to find immediately the most advanced treatments his profession had discovered. The mother, on the other hand, felt it would be best to apply all natural treatments. As she related to me the debate between her and her husband, it was evident that neither was willing to give in, and in their anxiety to help the child they were straining their relationship. They later both admitted that an increased level of anxiety in the home would only make it more difficult for the child. A requisite for any successful treatment is a healthy home environment, and this would be at risk if things continued in the direction they were going.

The devil himself must have originated the axiom "Divide and conquer." Although the enemy knows that trouble can either break us or make us stronger, he's learned he will almost always break us if he can cause division. This is true not only in the home but also in the church and even in society at large.

Our family's experiences through the years have tended to strengthen our marriage—not because we've necessarily agreed at every point along the way, but because we haven't allowed the little differences over details to ruin the big picture we share. More often than not, when I've felt discouraged, my wife has felt encouraged and so has encouraged me. And when she's felt discouraged, I've felt encouraged and have been able to encourage her.

At this point you may be thinking that this isn't a book about saving children, but rather about saving parents. I'm glad you noticed! The loss of one member of the family can precipitate the loss of others. While the devil works to keep our children from the Lord, he's also losing no time in trying to cause us parents to become discouraged. He does this by not only attacking us at the point of our weaknesses but also at the point of our strengths.

How easy it is for even our strong parental instincts to become corrupted. Love can become possessiveness. Long-suffering, leniency, mercy, can become indulgence; and steadfastness, rigidity. We may actually get to the point where we deeply resent those whom we love the most.

Often we may wonder why God doesn't just get this over with and answer our prayers to save our children right now. Aside from factors having to do with freedom of the will, God sees not just our children's needs but also our own. As we colabor with the Lord in the salvation of our children, the Holy Spirit is able to make necessary changes in our own lives. What a shame it would be if, in the end, our wayward children were saved and we were lost! Paul seems to have had a sense of this when he wrote: "But I keep under my body, and bring it into subjection: lest that by any means, when I have preached to others, I myself should be a cast-away" (1 Cor. 9:27).

Only a few homes have not been affected by divorce. From a grandparent's point of view, the pain of our children's divorces is augmented by how it impacts the grandchildren. In another chapter I'll relate to you lessons I learned from raising a granddaughter. But for the moment, I'd like for us to consider our grandchildren's parents who are no longer related to us by marriage. (This, of course, is a polite way of referring to our former sons- and daughters-in-law.)

A friend of mine once confessed she felt furious with her parents because they were still friends with her former husband. The situation leading up to the divorce had been particularly painful, and she interpreted the fact that her parents were still civil to the former spouse as disloyalty and a sign they didn't care for her.

For a moment I didn't know what to say, but then it occurred to me. I called her by name and said, "You must not forget, your mom and dad didn't divorce your husband—you did."

Though a divorce terminates a marriage, it doesn't terminate parenthood. I may no longer be someone's father-in-law, but I'll always be the grandfather. This means that as I pray that God will save my children and grandchildren, I must not forget to include the other parent. This can be difficult, especially if the other parent has little to do with spiritual things, or is even working against what we are praying God will do in the life of the child.

Have you ever read on the side of the tube of toothpaste what it's made of? Usually there's a line that says, "Active Ingredients." Then follows a list of chemicals that, not having studied chemistry, I can hardly pronounce.

The Christian life has its own active ingredients, and two

of the main ones are repentance and forgiveness. Repentance we will consider later, but for now I'd like to consider the implications of forgiveness. The forgiveness I'm referring to isn't the forgiveness of God toward us, but rather the forgiveness God has called on us to give to those who have wronged us or even sinned against us.

The model for forgiveness is Jesus' prayer: "Father, forgive them; for they know not what they do" (Luke 23:34). In some ways it's easier to admit we're wrong than it is to forgive those who have wronged us. When we think about the subject of forgiveness, two questions immediately surface. First, Why should we pray that God will help us forgive someone who isn't sorry? Second, If we pray for the gift of forgiveness, won't it mean that we approve of what others have done?

These questions must be resolved, or we simply will not ask for the gift of forgiveness. And if we don't ask, it will be impossible for us to be able to relate correctly to our children, their former spouses, and our grandchildren.

If we're to pray for the salvation of our grandchildren, we must also pray for both their parents, no matter who we might consider to be at fault.

Too often we pray generically. We say, "Lord, bless this one and bless that one." But what should you say when you don't believe the person you're thinking about ought to be blessed, such as an erring former daughter-in-law? You can't pray, "Lord, don't bless them." Just what should you say?

I was chatting with someone who had been through a bitter experience and, as a result, was full of resentment. I asked, "Do you ever pray for that other person?"

The response came through clinched teeth, "I sure do. I pray God will give them what they deserve."

I must confess that on occasion I, too, have felt that way, but I know this attitude isn't compatible with what I'm praying the Holy Spirit will do in my own life. In a family situation it can be the hardest thing in the world to forgive those who we thought loved us. If they really loved us, they wouldn't have done these things.

With tongue in cheek I often tell a listening congregation that it's not hard to love your enemies, provided they live in Antarctica. But if it means we must love an estranged husband or wife, a son or a daughter, or their spouses, this can be quite another matter. It's often easier to forgive a foreign dictator than to forgive relatives for wrongs they may have committed against us or our family.

What shall we do? Did Jesus forgive His enemies so that we wouldn't have to forgive ours? Or did He forgive us and, by doing so, instruct us: "For if ye forgive men their trespasses, your heavenly Father will also forgive you: but if ye forgive not men their trespasses, neither will your Father forgive your trespasses" (Matt. 6:14, 15)?

Earlier I mentioned taking physical therapy for adhesive capsulitis. Although the treatments were extremely painful, I had to submit to them. If I was going to regain movement in my arm, I had to stay on the table while the therapist did what had to be done. Sometimes, when I realize how sin has disabled us and what the gospel must do to break the power of anger, guilt, bitterness, pride, and selfishness in our lives, I want to cry out, "Lord, You're killing me, but keep it up!"

You see, anger, guilt, bitterness, pride, and selfishness can prevent us from standing in the gap when our children need us so badly. Once when Israel left the Lord, He cried, "And I sought for a man among them, that should make up the hedge, and stand in the gap before me for the land, that I should not destroy it: but I found none" (Eze. 22:30).

That may have happened in the time of Israel, but it must not happen now. Just as the umbilical cord nourished our children before they were born, so now we must serve as an umbilical cord that connects them with God. Just as a person in an intensive-care unit is kept alive by a life-support system, so our prayers are the life-support system for our children until they once again begin to pray for themselves.

Our family is learning the meaning of unconditional love, which is not always warm and cuddly. It loves in the face of apparent rejection. I've come to the conclusion that Jesus loves me not because of who I am but because that is the way He is. I want the Holy Spirit to make me like that too. Finally I'm beginning to realize that unconditional love is not so much about the one who is loved but about the one who loves. I want to be that kind of parent, a parent who loves no matter what.

CONSIDER THESE THINGS

1. God was forgiving before there was anyone to forgive. That is the way He is.
2. Having problems with our children can weaken our marriage or strengthen it.
3. God not only wants to save our children, but also wants to make sure we are saved in the process.
4. We must pray for former daughters-in-law and sons-in-law.
5. We should forgive those who have wronged us, because we need to be forgiven for our own sins.

DISCUSS WITH SOMEONE

1. Why must we not allow ourselves to be divorced from our grandchildren's parents?
2. How can our parental strong points become our weaknesses?

A PRAYER FROM THE HEART

Heavenly Father, we recognize that when we have problems in the family it can badly divide us or, worse still, cause us to turn away from You. We are thankful that while the devil tries to divide and conquer, You are calling on us as families to be united so that we can be healed. We recognize that even our strengths can become corrupted as we pass through trials. Lord, You know what the whole family needs. Help us trust that You see a bigger picture than we do.

We ask You to give us a spirit of forgiveness. We confess we may at times be bitter and angry at a former son- or daughter-in-law. Father, we pray for Your forgiveness and ask that You will also do in their lives all that we are praying for You to do in ours. We are sorry for the times we may not have provided them with the best example.

Father, when we begin to get a glimpse of our great need of new attitudes, we wonder how You will ever change us. Give us the strength not to try to run away from the work that You are doing in our hearts, although at times it seems painful.

Thank You for being a God of love. We want to be like You. Amen.

EIGHT

HOW TO LOOK BACK
WITHOUT GOING BACKWARD—1

"We cannot live only for ourselves. A thousand fibers con-nect us with our fellow men; and among those fibers, as sym-pathetic threads, our actions run as causes, and they come back to us as effects."—Herman Melville.

In order to be able to drive safely and especially to advance in traffic, it's necessary to have a rearview mirror. In fact, it's preferable to have several—one for each side and, of course, the middle one stuck to the windshield that reflects what is going on directly behind the car. One day as I was traveling down the interstate, it occurred to me how danger-ous it would be if we didn't have mirrors. Strategically placed mirrors allow us to look back and to the sides and still focus on going forward.

The mirrors on the sides of the car are especially inter-esting. Usually printed in the corner of the passenger's side mirror are the words: "Objects in mirror are closer than they appear." The mirror on the driver's side actually has a blind spot. To compensate, I've added a little fish-eye mirror.

Experienced drivers learn how to back up using rearview mirrors. This is effective for parking or preparing to unload a truck, but to attempt to go forward on the interstate using only the mirrors is out of the question.

There can be no doubt that where we're going in life is heavily influenced by where we've been. Who I am today is the result of who I was yesterday. Our lives are to a great extent molded by the law of cause and effect. Every action will have a corresponding reaction.

When a couple marries, they may think that they're starting a brand-new home, and in one sense they are. But the truth is, each brings to the marriage bits of the homes from which he or she has come, and the new family is new only in the sense that it represents a new merger of two older families.

Within the law of cause and effect there operates another law, the law of influence. That law simply means we become like what we look at. The significance that this has for a family is that unless we do something intentional, we'll become like our parents. In computer language we'd say that our default setting is our parents. In a sinless environment this might have been acceptable, but 6,000 years down the line it can complicate your life!

The Ten Commandments point out the problem: "For I the Lord thy God am a jealous God, visiting the iniquity of the fathers upon the children unto the third and fourth generation of them that hate me" (Ex. 20:5).

In other words, when the sins of our forebears get on a roll, they're very difficult to stop and will have multigenerational consequences. If this is the way it has to be, we might throw up our hands and wonder if there's hope for any of us.

This chapter and the one that follows are about looking back. As in the example of driving a car, we cannot go forward in our lives unless we are aware of where we've been. There's a way to look back and have a wreck, and there's a way to look back and *avoid* having a wreck.

We must learn to look back without going backward. When we've learned to do this, it will help us understand who we are and where we are coming from. And as we pray that God will save our children, it will help us understand what we may at times expect of them.

I heard an interesting story about a young Christian man whose father was an alcoholic. Over time people began to comment on how the boy seemed to become more and more like his father. This did not mean the young man began to drink or stopped attending church. You see, a particular lifestyle results from certain attitudes. Although the boy didn't have the bad habits of his father, he did have the same type of character. It has been my experience that we become more like our parents as we get older. I noticed that I'd become more like my dad when I was 55 than when I was 35. I thank God for the influence my dad made on me. I've finally reached the place where I can see my dad's positive as well as negative impact in my life.

We thank God that He used our parents to create us, but, using computer jargon, we would be wise to go to Preferences, then to Settings, and there choose the positive elements for our lives that we didn't get naturally from our parents. While we're there it may also be necessary to "uncheck" some of the negative elements we picked up. It's important that we do this not with resentment but with the confidence that God is able to take each of us where we are and make us into His image.

I was a role model for my children. I was a positive role model in some things and a negative role model in others. By default our children have absorbed both the positive and the negative.

Although our children are grown, I'm nevertheless still impacting their lives in important ways. Our influence over our children is never ending, and for this reason it's never too late for us to look in the rearview mirror to see where we have come from, because it will prove invaluable in helping us know where we are heading.

As I look in the rearview mirror of my life, I can see that I didn't listen very carefully. I mostly operated on the basis that the squeaky wheel gets the grease, and if it isn't squeaking it doesn't need anything. Even now I have a problem listening. It has been said that we men tend to be problem solvers. Just tell us the problem, and we'll immediately try to solve it. Our problem is that we often jump to conclusions and try to solve the problem before we know the details.

At times I was more interested in the product than in the process. I wanted a solution no matter the cost. As a result, I could easily be insensitive to the feelings of others and would also be a setup for the old saying "A person persuaded against his will is of the same opinion still."

Our children and grandchildren, and for that matter our spouses, have the right to expect that we'll be consistent and that we'll practice what we preach. Some years ago I was invited to conduct a weekend revival. My host met me curbside at the airport. As I climbed into the car, the first thing I noticed was that he had a radar detector. He said he had some errands to run before we headed home and asked if I would mind accompanying him.

Although we hadn't known each other before, it wasn't long before he was sharing with me some of what was going on in his life. The weekend before my arrival his teenage son had gotten with some of the other young people in the church and had decided on the spur of the moment to engage in some light delinquency; namely, they went into a community and threw raw eggs at the neighbors' houses. They got caught, and now my new friend was rightly concerned as to the direction his son's life seemed to be heading.

I listened sympathetically, asking a question from time to time, but other than that made little comment. The following day, as we got into the car, my attention again focused on the radar detector. As we rode along I casually referenced what his boy had done and asked, "Have you ever considered that there might be a linkage between this radar detector and what your boy and his friends did to those houses the other night?"

I pointed out that a radar detector can be construed as a statement that one intends to break the law. Not a big important law, just the one that declares that the speed limit on the interstate is 70 mph. The young people that night did not consider throwing eggs on houses anything big or serious. They were just out for a good time mixed with a little adrenaline.

Looking back through the rearview mirror, it's not hard to see how sometimes what we consider to be acceptable adult behavior, when interpreted at the next level down in the family chain, can result in making us very uncomfortable and even concerned.

Although we miss the bull's-eye at times, we don't have to miss it every time. I often find myself looking back through the rearview mirror, not so that I'll go backward but so that 30 years down the road I can avoid the same pitfalls I experience now. If there aren't any perfect people, then how can there be perfect parents? But we can wish that we were, and must continue to make every effort to meet the high standard God has set before us.

Although the Bible specifically tells us not to judge each other, it does call on us to judge ourselves: "For if we would judge ourselves, we should not be judged. But when we are judged, we are chastened of the Lord, that we should not be condemned with the world" (1 Cor. 11:31, 32).

Some of us may not feel comfortable with this concept, because on the surface it seems to be a call to put ourselves down, which could be hard on one's self-esteem. But I believe the text makes a lot of sense. I'd rather discover on my own that my shirttail is hanging out than have someone else point it out to me!

Everyone, especially members of the family, are well aware of my faults and foibles. The sooner I get on board, the better it will be for everyone. Quiet time in the morning is the best time for what might be called a self-audit. When I'm alone with God, realizing that He loves me and I love Him, the experience of looking at my faults and failures isn't threatening. On the contrary, it can be like pulling into a car wash and getting rid of the things that have tended to take the shine out of life.

Making a morning audit a practice tends to keep one up-to-date. My self-audit rarely has to go back further than yesterday. I'll purposely think of the important things that happened yesterday and determine if they were consistent with what I would want them to be today. Now and again I see certain recurring patterns that need to be taken into account, and at that time Jesus and I will talk about it.

To some this may sound like righteousness by works. Actually, it's the way righteousness works. Although I wish I were the kind of husband and father who never made mistakes, along the way I want to learn from my mistakes. Realizing that I make mistakes will help me not to be surprised when others do the same, and if I expect Jesus to be patient with me in my mistakes, I must learn to be patient with others in theirs.

Exodus 20:5 says that God will visit the iniquities of the fathers upon the children unto the third and fourth generation of them that hate Him, but we must not stop reading there. We don't happen to be among those that hate Him. *We are those who love Him.* The text has good news for us, because verse 6 adds: "And shewing mercy unto thousands of them that love me, and keep my commandments."

That is us! Despite the fact we weren't always what we ought to have been, the good news is that we are not yet what we will be (1 John 3:2). When our children grew up and moved away, they took with them some of our strengths and our weaknesses. Unfortunately, human nature being the way it is, they'll more likely emulate our weaknesses than our strengths.

There may be parents reading this book who themselves were prodigal sons or daughters when raising their family, and they might think that God will hold them responsible for how the children turned out.

I found a passage of Scripture that explains how God looks at us: "The son shall not bear the iniquity of the father, neither shall the father bear the iniquity of the son: the righteousness of the righteous shall be upon him, and the wickedness of the wicked shall be upon him. But if the wicked will turn from all his sins that he hath committed, and keep all my statutes, and do that which is lawful and right, he shall surely live, he shall not die. All his transgressions that he hath committed, they shall not be mentioned unto him: in his righteousness that he hath done he shall live" (Eze. 18:20-22).

The ground at the foot of the cross is level. For those who love God, His grace gets us beyond our past, and through the power of the indwelling Spirit we press on toward the mark of the high calling of God in Christ Jesus (Phil. 3:14).

CONSIDER THESE THINGS

1. If we are to drive safely forward, we must occasionally look backward. And so in our lives unless we see where we have come from, we cannot know where we are headed.

2. Those who don't learn from the mistakes of the past

are bound to repeat them.

3. We will tend to emulate our parents. If we are to be different from them, it must be intentional.
4. I can be respectful of my parents in spite of negative characteristics they may have.
5. In the judgment, people are accountable for their own actions.

DISCUSS WITH SOMEONE

1. Talk candidly about some negative things you did in the past that can actually help you to be stronger now.
2. Identify some little "radar detectors" in your life that may be giving others the wrong example.

A PARENT'S PRAYER

Holy Father, You were with me in the past even when I wasn't paying attention. Even though in my foolish past I did things that I wouldn't do again, I know that You don't hold them against me and that You are with me even now. Lord, You know the burden I have for the children. Sometimes I can see that they are just like me when I was their age. Help me understand that just as You changed me so You can change them, and that I need not fear for the future except as I forget the way You have been with us despite our past. In Jesus' name, amen.

HOW TO LOOK BACK
WITHOUT GOING BACKWARD—2

"Life can be real tough. . . . You can either learn from your problems or keep repeating them over and over."
—Marie Osmond.

While I attended academy and college I worked for a plastering contractor. I'll always be thankful for that job, not only because it made it possible for me to earn my way through school, but also because it made me appreciate the importance of the building trades and reminded me that Jesus was a carpenter.

During the summer months when there was a lot of work to be done, it wasn't unusual to begin the day's work at 7:00 a.m. and still be on the job at 6:00 p.m. I mixed and carried the plaster. By the end of the day I often felt so tired I could hardly stand up.

Often the boss would not be on the job when we began but would arrive around 4:00 p.m. With enthusiasm he'd pick up his hock and trowel and say, "All right, boys, let's go to work!"

Right! We *had* been working since early morning. Once in a while one of us would respond, "We've been here all day working. Where were you?"

His answer has stayed with me through the years. "There's more to plastering than simply putting it on the wall."

Likewise, there's more to the salvation of our children and grandchildren than praying, "Lord, keep Your mansions—just save my children." An important element is our personal relationship with the Lord and also with them. In saving our children God has to start somewhere, and it might as well be with us!

In chapter 7 we learned about two active ingredients—repentance and forgiveness—in the Christian life. In this chapter we'll consider repentance (and confession).

It's difficult to discuss this subject with people who either feel that they've done nothing wrong or that if they did something wrong it was someone else's fault. To repent is to admit we made a mistake and to make a commitment to do the right thing in the future. Some get nervous when it comes to admitting mistakes. They have the impression that if you admit you made a mistake, people will lose respect for you. Actually, it's just the other way around: "He that covereth his sins shall not prosper: but whoso *confesseth and forsaketh* them shall have mercy" (Prov. 28:13).

It's easy to confess mistakes, provided they aren't your own! Sometimes we've become so accustomed to doing something a particular way that we may actually not be aware that what we're doing is unacceptable.

One afternoon I was walking through the grounds of a large building. The men who cared for the lawns were cutting the grass. I stopped to greet them, and we began talking about spiritual things. In the course of the conversation one of those men said something I shall never forget: "Pastor, listen to what your enemies have to say about you. They will often tell you things about yourself your friends would be afraid to say."

If we're wise we will be alert to hear—from whatever the source—that which, if we are honest with ourselves, can help us grow as Christians.

One evening as we were having worship with our little granddaughter, after Grandma had finished reading a story, we knelt to pray. As we prayed it dawned on me that what we were saying amounted to "Lord, help Andrea do this; help Andrea be that; forgive her for this; forgive her for that; and help Andrea be a good girl." Of course we weren't saying those exact words, but this was essentially the thought.

I can see now that when we pray that way with our children, they must flinch, because it is as if we were giving them a prayer spanking! Perhaps there would be no problem if we would only include ourselves in the prayer. When we pray, "Jesus, help _____," they should also hear us say, "Jesus, help Grandpa and Grandma be kind and loving."

It's difficult to teach our children and grandchildren to admit they have made mistakes if they have never seen such behavior modeled. How can they learn to say, "Please forgive me," if they have never heard us say the words?

I'm now making an effort to be the parent and grandparent—30 years later—that I ought to have been previously. Sometimes my grown children have reminded me of negative things I did when I was a young parent. Although I can't go back, I do feel bad and take the opportunity to ask their forgiveness.

Some years ago there was a popular sentiment: "Love means never having to say 'I'm sorry.'" Nothing could be further from the truth. True love is about being able to admit when we have wronged those we love and to ask their forgiveness. Our relationship with the One who loves us most is the template for this. In 1 John 1:9 we are told that if we confess our sins, He is faithful and just to forgive us and to cleanse us from all unrighteousness.

Inasmuch as we wrong each other, there comes a time when cleansing is in order. Although we are commanded to forgive even if the other doesn't ask for forgiveness, there comes a time in which relationships are all too often set back for lack of the words "I was wrong. Will you please forgive me?"

It may come as a surprise to some, but there's a way to ask, and a way not to ask, for forgiveness. Suppose a mother is cleaning up the kitchen. She asks her teenage son, who is at the kitchen table doing his homework, if he would mind taking out the kitchen trash. He's in the middle of a math problem and responds, "Can't you see I'm trying to study? How do you expect me to finish my homework if you interrupt me all the time?"

Gathering his books, he storms out and stomps to his room to finish the assignment. A while later he thinks about what he has done and decides he needs to apologize to his mother. "Mom, I'm sorry I didn't take out the trash."

Now it's Mom's turn. "Son, I don't know what I'm going to do with you. You don't do anything I ask you to do anymore. And your room is a mess!"

The young man's face turns red. Again he storms out of the room, thinking this will be the last time he tells Mom he's sorry for anything. Obviously, the mother should not have reacted the way she did, but let's rewind this scenario and consider another option.

Instead of apologizing for not carrying out the trash, suppose he'd said something like "Mom, I recognize I haven't been doing my part around the house lately. I really appreciate all you do, and I want to ask your forgiveness. Will you forgive me, Mom?"

Often when we ask for forgiveness, we fall short of recognizing or admitting what actually was at the root of the problem. The wrongs we commit against each other, perhaps without our meaning to, often have their roots in selfishness, lack of appreciation, taking someone for granted, or just plain being unkind.

Have you heard the latest generic apology, "Sorry 'bout

that"? These words can hardly be passed off as representing a sincere desire to make things right with one we may have hurt. Imagine that I step on your foot. You say, "Ouch!" I say, "Sorry 'bout that."

You might be tempted to say, "Sorry 'bout what? Sorry I was in your way?" When we ask someone to forgive us, often it isn't enough just to say, "I'm sorry."

Another way not to apologize is to say, "I was wrong, but you were wrong too." This method is not so much a confession as it is an accusation.

Also, when trying to make things right, avoid saying, "I'm sorry if I have a done anything to offend you." The question easily comes to the mind of the other person, *And you don't know what you did?*

Perhaps the weakest confession is one in which we ask for forgiveness but then add, "The reason I did that was that . . ." The other person might rightfully think, *I hope those circumstances don't arise again, or he's implying that he might do it again!*

A better confession might be "I realize I've been selfish in my attitude toward you. [Identify the attitude that caused the action—unkindness, dishonesty, ungratefulness, jealousy, lack of respect, etc.] Will you please forgive me?"

Some people feel that expressing sorrow for what they have done eliminates the need for an apology. But let's put it another way: If I'm truly sorry, then why not apologize? Jesus Himself spoke to this point when He said, "Therefore if thou bring thy gift to the altar, and there rememberest that thy brother hath ought against thee; leave there thy gift before the altar, and go thy way; first be reconciled to thy brother, and then come and offer thy gift" (Matt. 5:23, 24).

Although we cannot do the work of the Holy Spirit in another person's heart, nevertheless for our part we are admonished: "If it be possible, as much as lieth in you, live peaceably with all men" (Rom. 12:18).

Few things are more frustrating than a computer that keeps coming up with an error message or that continually crashes. When this happens we don't usually sit helplessly by. We call the computer support department, the factory, a buddy, or anyone who will help us solve the problem. Not only do we insist on a computer doing what it's supposed to do, but also we often decide that our particular model has become obsolete, and so we purchase new equipment that is literally up to speed.

I wish we were as sensitive in our relationships with God and with those we love as we are in the high-tech areas of our lives. How many times, particularly when I first began to work with a computer, did I call technical support? I have waited on hold for up to a half hour and even stayed up until midnight trying to solve a problem with the software or the operating system. What would our family relationships and our relationship with God be like if we persevered with them as we do with our computers?

The Bible tells the story of a man who persevered with God. "And Jacob was left alone; and there wrestled a man with him until the breaking of the day. And when he saw that he prevailed not against him, he touched the hollow of his thigh; and the hollow of Jacob's thigh was out of joint, as he wrestled with him. And he said, Let me go, for the day breaketh. And he said, I will not let thee go, except thou bless me. And he said unto him, What is thy name? And he said, Jacob. And he said, Thy name shall be called no more Jacob, but Israel: for as a prince hast thou power with God and with men, and hast prevailed" (Gen. 32:24-28).

Jacob went to prayer that night thinking his biggest problem was that his brother was about to take revenge on him and his family. As the night wore on, he began to realize the part that he had played in all that had gone on, and soon he was more interested in getting victory over *Jacob* than over Esau, his brother.

The purpose of prayers for children and ourselves is not to convince God that He needs to save them or us. "But God commendeth his love toward us, in that, while we were yet sinners, Christ died for us" (Rom. 5:8). Those whom God saves must allow themselves a change of heart.

We wish our children were in church every week, but God wishes so even more. He wishes that we and our children would allow Him to change us and them *completely*. The problem is not our struggle with God, but rather it is His struggle with us. Once we realize who the problem is, we'll be more inclined to cry out in our brokenness, "We will not let You go unless You bless us." When we do that, He will bless us.

CONSIDER THESE THINGS

1. We must be careful not to pray *at* our children.
2. Human nature resists admitting when it has done wrong.
3. We will change what we do when we identify and confess the attitudes that motivate us.
4. When we are truly repentant, we will do all in our power to make things right.
5. We are often more concerned that our computers run right than we are that our relationships with our loved ones are right.

DISCUSS WITH SOMEONE

1. What are some of the most common attitudes that cloud our relationships with our loved ones?

2. Why does true love make asking forgiveness important?

A PARENT'S PRAYER

Dear God, we are thankful that You have promised if we confess our sins, You are faithful and just to forgive us and to cleanse us from all unrighteousness. Sometimes we wrong others—especially those we love. We do this even without meaning to. Teach us how to make things right with each other so there will be nothing that would cloud our relationships. We know You are not trying to put us down; rather You want to lift us up. Impress our hearts as to how to say just the right words at the right times to our children. We don't want them to use us as an excuse for not coming to You. Thank You for hearing our prayer. Amen.

TEN

WHO'S IN CHARGE HERE?

"The art of being wise is the art of knowing what to overlook."—William James.

When I see parents with young children, I remember our own little flock. We traveled together by air, sea, and land—literally. Frankly, I don't see how we did it. In more recent years as I travel overseas, I stay in the homes of missionaries from time to time. Sometimes I think to myself that if I were them I'd never take my family to some far-off land. I forget that this is exactly what we did.

When we are young we tend to be more adventuresome than we are later in life. Betty and I felt called to the mission field and never regretted the years we spent away from our homeland. In terms of quantity they were probably the leanest years of our lives, but in terms of quality they provided some of our best memories despite war, revolution, and economic depression.

When you take four children to a country in which a revolution is brewing, you'd better be in charge. You can't afford to leave anything to chance. In preparing to set up housekeeping somewhere remote for a period of years, you learn what is essential and what you can do without. Inasmuch as overweight baggage could cost a dollar a pound, we tried to carry as much as we possibly could on our persons. On one occasion this necessitated rehearsing in the hotel room how we'd get on the plane!

When you're in a new country with a new language and a new culture, the family unit tends to be solid. We stick together because we're all we've got. At one point the country in which we were living was on the verge of civil war. As the political crisis deepened we advised the children that one day they might go to school and not be able to get home. But they were not to worry, because someone would take care of them. We didn't know who that someone might be, but we wanted to prepare them for whatever might happen. We wanted them to understand that they didn't need to worry, because we had foreseen all the possibilities. We were in control.

Being in control is what being a parent of young children is all about. Control and responsibility go together. If I'm responsible for something, I must be in control. But it is precisely here that problems begin to arise.

As parents we are 100 percent responsible for our children when they are small. As they mature and develop, responsibility shifts, and of course, the type of and degree of control we exercise over them changes.

One of the most difficult aspects of parenting is not just that we learn how and when to lessen our control, but also that they as adults, with the freedom they now enjoy, must not infringe on our freedom and responsibilities. In other words, if we are not to control our adult children, neither must we find ourselves being controlled by them.

One of our children complained to me that Mother had a point of view they considered unfair. I explained that inasmuch as they are entitled to feel a certain way about a particular matter, they must give the same right to their parents, in this case to Mother. The young person confessed they'd not thought of it that way before.

A sensitive area when dealing with grown children has to

do with faith and morals. On the one hand, we parents must not try to do what God Himself refuses to do—impose our religious beliefs on them. On the other hand, it would not be consistent that unbelieving children impose their particular lifestyles on their parents. If when we go to visit them we must respect their way of life, it only stands to reason that when they come to visit us they should respect the lifestyle that they themselves may no longer practice.

It's not unusual that adult children may feel they have a right to live the way they please while enjoying the hospitality of their parents. Their argument may be that because they entered adulthood their parents can no longer tell them what they can or cannot do. This way of thinking may create tension in the home. None should forget that hospitality is not a one-way street.

It is difficult to discuss this topic because of the many subjective elements involved, yet I believe there are principles that, if pursued, can improve situations that may have developed and, when implemented, can even avert future problems.

When we raised our children, we tried to adhere to certain principles. For instance, we'd explain to them why we did a certain thing a certain way. In the mind of the children this gave a religious significance to what we were doing. With the passing of years the young people may have given up the religion and the lifestyle that accompanied it. Inasmuch as we can no longer control their spiritual lives, they may take this to mean that now they don't have to respect our lifestyle any longer.

At this point we must be as wise as serpents and as harmless as doves. The tendency will be to remonstrate with them based on what we believe is right and wrong. Immediately tensions will arise, because they have rejected for the time being our spiritual values.

While we have surrendered one type of control, there is that responsibility and control which cannot be delegated or surrendered and for which we must stand firm. This means that instead of establishing norms for living in the home from a perspective of "right" and "wrong," we must change our approach.

One day I was talking with my son, who by now was almost 20, about guidelines for living at home. I explained to him that we had to have rules for living together and that I couldn't think of anywhere a person could live where there wouldn't be at least some minimum house rules.

At this time of his life his values were in a state of flux. I explained that I understood we didn't share the same standards anymore but that I would appreciate it if he would respect mine, not because he necessarily agreed with them from a religious point of view but for my sake as his father. I knew he still loved me, and I was appealing not to his respect for the church but to his respect for me as his father. But even then there were times when who was in charge in the house became an issue.

Miraculously, all four of our children eventually became perfect housekeepers, but it wasn't always that way. Although two were usually neat, the other two at times kept rooms that looked like a pigpen. Maybe I should have ignored it, but a room with the shades drawn, the door always closed, and the inside becoming a public health nuisance doesn't increase the value of the real estate!

So one day, seeing that things were not getting any better, I asked my son to clean his room. The reply was polite and positive; that's the good news. The bad news is that the room didn't get cleaned. A day or two later I again asked him to clean the room, this time with deep sincerity. Again I was assured it would be done, but again it wasn't.

Now the issue ratcheted up to the next level. No longer was it just about a neat room, but about my right as his resident "dean of men" to ask him to straighten it up. I began to dig in, and needless to say, what had before been polite discussion began to become somewhat tense.

Later I realized that instead of losing on one front, I was beginning to lose on two. Not only did I still have a room that was, from my perspective, becoming a public health menace, but also my relationship with this young adult was beginning to unravel. I then had to decide on my next move. Would I press this to a showdown over who was in charge, or would I give up and accept the messy room? I decided to do neither.

When someone asks whether you prefer to do "this" or "that," it can be the better part of wisdom to ask for another option. The most apparent choices may not be the best ones. In this case I decided to do something completely different.

I decided I didn't have to be a two-time loser—lose communication with my son and end up with a messy room to boot. I decided I'd clean the room myself, and so I did. Nothing was said, so I cleaned it the next day, too. Guess what? Without saying anything he cleaned it the third day, and so it went. It wasn't long before he kept the room fairly clean, and our relationship remained intact. That incident did not result in all of our problems disappearing, but at least it didn't make things worse.

At times I've wondered whatever happened to the soft, cuddly little ones we once knew. We might as well get used to it—those days are gone. A person who works in an institution for the mentally ill told about a time he was talking with one of the patients. The patient tried to explain that it was not easy to be emotionally disturbed. Finally he pointed to his head and said, "Be patient with us. We are still in here."

I have often thought of that when times were hard. What happened to our obedient, loving little ones? I don't know, but we must be patient because they are still in there . . . somewhere!

God is patient with us, and He has called on us to be patient with each other. To be patient doesn't mean we must compromise our principles. Even though our grown children may seem to push us to compromise, in their heart of hearts they're hoping we won't. With their lives often in a state of flux, even if they don't happen to agree at the moment, it can be comforting to know that Mom and Dad can be counted on to be stable.

"Wisdom is better than weapons of war: but one sinner destroyeth much good" (Eccl. 9:18). Although our responsibilities as parents of maturing or mature children may not include the same control it did when they were little, yet the responsibilities we now have are in many ways just as important.

The day our eldest daughter married, Betty sighed, "Well, that's one less to worry about."

Wrong! As our children have married one by one, our concerns haven't decreased but have actually increased as their families grew. And although our roles have changed, our responsibilities as parents continue.

For years I've worked as a director of Community Services, and before that with ADRA. Over time I've developed the philosophy that we ought not to help the needy as much as we can but as little as is necessary for them to be able to help themselves.

It's unavoidable—there are always strings attached to assistance, and that means control. It wasn't God's plan that we control each other but that we encourage each other and, where necessary, provide that which is essential for a person to become independent.

The more we materially help our grown children, the more we will feel we have the right to control what they do. And the more we control them, the more they will seek to manipulate us.

We should not seek to control, yet we have responsibilities to our children. Not the same responsibilities as when they were young, but important ones nonetheless for this time of our lives and theirs.

CONSIDER THESE THINGS

1. Children expect their parents to respect their points of view.
2. The above being true, children must respect their parents' convictions.
3. We can win a battle and lose the war, but we can also lose a battle and finally win the war.
4. Our homes should reflect our values, and those who live with us should respect them for our sakes.
5. The more we provide material help to others, the more we feel the right to participate in their decisions.

DISCUSS WITH SOMEONE

1. Is it possible to help a person too much?
2. How can we explain our values to others without making them feel intimidated if they do not agree?

A PARENT'S PRAYER

Father in heaven, we have tried to raise our children according to the principles that You have given us. Now they seem to have turned their backs on what they learned. Lord, we know we cannot communicate with them as we did when they were little children. Sometimes we say the wrong things, and they seem not to want to listen anymore. You said that if we needed wisdom we should ask You for it, and so we are doing that now. Help us know how to speak the truth in love so that when they hear, they will remember the things they learned. And may the Holy Spirit convict their hearts. Amen.

ELEVEN

KNOWING WHEN TO LET GO

"She who loves roses must be patient and not cry out when she is pierced by thorns."—Olga Brouman.

There are many mysteries we cannot understand. Even if they were explained to us, we wouldn't understand! Understanding comes from experience and observation, which are limited for everyone. There's no greater mystery than the mystery of the human heart. While physical sciences are predictable, things having to do with human behavior, although observable and chartable, are nevertheless often unpredictable.

Why one third of the angels, living in God's personal presence, decided that His government was not for them can only be described as a mystery. Scripture describes the human heart in its natural condition: "The heart is deceitful above all things, and desperately wicked: who can know it?" (Jer. 17:9).

We often speak of "innocent little children." A parent described how one day his 2-year-old son was in the high chair, eating a bowl of cereal. He told the child to be careful not to push the cereal off onto the floor. He said he'll never forget how the child looked him straight in the eye as he deliberately put his little hands around the bowl and pushed it off the edge. Innocent? Sometimes we wonder! "Even a child is known by his doings, whether his work be pure, and whether it be right" (Prov. 20:11).

We have a parakeet named Baby Cakes. We purchased him from a pet store when he was just learning to eat by himself. He was easy to tame. He quickly learned to say, "Happy Sabbath," "I'm a silly bird," and "Where's Andrea?" No one ever taught him how to be a parakeet, yet he does just fine. Animals are that way. Take a kitten away from its mother at 8 weeks of age, and it may never see another cat as long as it lives, yet its built-in "software" makes it a cat.

Human beings may have a hard drive and an operating system, but their lives will depend to a large degree on the types of programs their environment "installs" as they go along. Humans have the potential to be either something lower than an animal or something akin to God Himself. Yet overriding the environment is that factor unique to humans —the power to choose. This is the part of us that relates to God and is the handle God uses to lift us up.

Parents play a large part in installing programs into the lives of children, but there comes a time when these programs must be bought into by the children themselves. This happens primarily during the teen years.

Earlier, I mentioned that I was raised in a minister's home. By today's standards it was conservative, but by today's standards most homes in those days tended to be conservative. My dad tore up the Sunday comics. We didn't eat meat, didn't go to movies, didn't wear jewelry, and didn't listen to "worldly music." Although everyone wasn't like us, I can't remember wishing that it were any other way.

From my earliest years I wanted to be a minister. Of course, I went through the stage of wanting to be a fireman and a cowboy, but those were only passing fancies. During my second year of college I began to wonder how the other half lived. I went to movies a few times, and I tasted meat.

(When you've never eaten meat before, it can be an interesting experience!)

Friday nights became the nights of my discontent. I felt restless and agitated. From my dormitory room I wondered what was going on out there in the world and began to have a desire to expand my horizons. One day I decided I would talk with Dean Loewen about some of my feelings.

I don't remember how I began the conversation, but finally I was able to tell him that I'd decided I wanted to taste something of what the world was all about. I went on and on with my threats and complaining, and I wondered what he might say. He listened patiently and quietly, and when I had finished he simply said, "Go ahead."

That wasn't exactly the answer I'd been waiting for. Wasn't he going to plead with me not to go? Wasn't he going to tell me how much I'd regret it? He didn't; he just told me to go ahead. I could do what I wanted. I walked out of his office thinking about what had just transpired. It was then I decided that I really didn't want to see what the world was all about. I liked my life the way it was.

Sooner or later what happened to me that day happens to everyone, but not always with the same result. Until that moment I was living my parents' values. They were not my values but theirs. I'd come to the place where I had to choose whether I was going to give them up or make them my own. When Dean Loewen said, "Go ahead," he was telling me that the choices my parents had made for me up to this stage of my development had expired and that the choices for the future were now mine.

Whether or not this occurs for others at age 18 as it did for me, sooner or later it must happen for everyone. Obviously, for some the transition is not smooth. Sometimes I tease teens by reminding them that if they want to prove they can drive, they don't do it by wrecking the car. But sadly for some, this is exactly what they do.

If you would have asked me a few years ago what kind of person I am when it comes to finances, I would have answered, "I'm a good money manager."

As the years have come and gone, though, I've become more and more aware that it would probably be more accurate to say that I am a tightwad—another word would be stingy. However, I married a generous girl. How a tightwad like me ended up marrying a generous person like her is beyond me—and probably beyond her, too!

She's not recklessly generous, mind you. Betty is very careful with money, but always generously thoughtful on birthdays and other special occasions. When Christmastime comes, she wants to plan gifts for everyone. Often when she finds something she thinks is pretty for the grandchildren, she asks me what I think about it. To me it's not how pretty it is or how much the children will like it, but how much it costs.

I'm ashamed to say that during the greater part of our married life, instead of learning to be generous like she is, I tried to make her stingy like I am. One day as we were riding together in the car, right out of the blue I asked my wife, "If I dropped dead, would you be happy?"

She must have thought I was out of my mind. This was not a question that came out of an argument, but it was a question that came from my own mind. Let me explain. You see, I travel quite a bit. Sometimes when I return home, I'll tell Betty what went on during the trip. Later when we're visiting her sisters, she might say, "Last Monday Dick was in Pittsburgh, and then on Tuesday he went to Chicago."

Wrong! I went to Chicago on Wednesday, not Tuesday, and so I correct her in midstory. I not only correct her but also take over telling the story. She politely becomes silent while I finish telling about whatever had happened.

It was this and other attempts to correct and change her that I was thinking about when I asked her if she'd be happy if I dropped dead. I could see I was wrong in the way I'd been treating her in this respect. After all, what difference did Tuesday or Wednesday make? She was only trying to share my life with me, and I was trying to tag her out on a technicality.

When I asked her if she'd be happy if I dropped dead, I was trying to say, "Am I keeping you from really being what God has meant for you to be?" What a wonderful thing it is that we're all different! And we need not only to allow for differences but also to encourage and affirm those differences. I'd been wrong in trying to make her stingy like me, and I decided then and there to set her free, free to be all that God meant for her to be. In doing this, my own life will be greatly enriched. I'm glad to report that since I made that decision my life has been the better, and I'm sure hers has been too! I'm still stingy, but not as much as before. Both God and Betty are making progress in my life.

Someone once said that when God made us, we were so unique that He said, "I don't think I'll do that again."

The most important challenges we face as parents are recognizing our children as unique personalities and resisting the temptation to make them like us or to be disappointed when they aren't. My father had two sons who became ministers. I had two sons, and neither chose to follow in my footsteps, yet I'm proud of them both.

One made his choices in life much as I did, while the other made his in storm and turmoil. But whether in tempest or in calm, children must make their own choices and buy into their own value systems, because it's the power of choice that makes us distinctly human.

Knowing how and when to let go is the challenge we face. Letting go doesn't mean we don't care anymore. When we let go and they don't do things the way we expect, we can come to the conclusion they don't love us, when actually they do.

It felt safer when they were little. We made their decisions for them and hoped that the decisions were the right ones. Now we must stop trying to make their decisions or feeling resentment when they don't do things the way we believe they ought to.

Paul speaks of a time for childhood and a time for adulthood. "When I was a child, I spake as a child, I understood as a child, I thought as a child: but when I became a man, I put away childish things" (1 Cor. 13:11). We may not have thought about it when they were young, but we were not so much raising children as we were raising future men and women, future parents and grandparents.

Now we must let go. They've made their choices for the time being. They may have made wrong choices, but such need not be the case forever. We ourselves have made wrong choices, and look what God has done for us. He has promised that He will never leave us or forsake us. The important thing is that while our children may waver, we ourselves must not waver. We must not lose our own trust in God. We need to affirm and reaffirm our personal commitment.

While our children make their own choices, we must be faithful to those we have made. "Choose you this day whom ye [our children] will serve; . . . but as for me and my house, we will serve the Lord" (Joshua 24:15). We must now step back in our children's lives, knowing that God won't.

CONSIDER THESE THINGS

1. Human nature is unpredictable.
2. No matter how correct we were in bringing up our chil-

dren, there comes a time when they must choose their own values.

3. Though our children may have, for the time being, bought into a new set of values, we should be as patient with them as God has been with us.
4. Each person is a distinct creation and, as such, has unique potential.
5. In trying to make others like us, we may be perpetuating our own weaknesses.

DISCUSS WITH SOMEONE

1. How can we be supportive of a person who is in the valley of decision?
2. How can we be a positive influence without appearing to be domineering?

A PARENT'S PRAYER

Dear Lord, I don't know how You are so patient with us. You have given us the wonderful power of choice, and we wish we always made the right choices. Thank You for not always interfering in our lives even when we get on the wrong track. How else can we learn the consequences of our decisions? But, Lord, when Satan asked for permission to test Job, You said he could do it but that he couldn't take his life. So we don't ask that You shield our children from all consequences, only that You please preserve their lives. We can't see the end from the beginning like You can, so we will have to trust that what You allow for any of us is just and right. We know we can say this, because You love us even more than we love those who are nearest and dearest to us. Give us the patience to continue to trust in You as Jesus did. We pray this in His name, amen.

TWELVE

WHEN YOU CAN'T SOLVE THE PROBLEM

"Kind words can be short and easy to speak, but their echoes are truly endless."—Mother Teresa.

Some years ago I was asked to speak at a Week of Prayer conducted by one of the churches in central California. On the first weekend someone asked if I would mind giving a chapel talk at the local day academy on Monday morning. I agreed that I would.

Speaking to teenagers is not my first choice of speaking appointments, although I make it a point never to turn down such an invitation. It can be a challenge to keep their interest and attention. Most young people are raised on TV and video games, and this has tended to hyperstimulate them.

Watching television doesn't help a person be a good listener. Of course, you really can't be a rude listener when you watch a TV program. You can talk, laugh, or walk out of the room, and the program goes on just the same, whereas being a listener in an audience requires respect and consideration for the speaker.

I knew I had to present something that would hold the young people's attention, so after I was introduced, I stood up and announced that I was going to give them three short seminars. I explained that businesspersons pay big money to attend seminars, especially when they're getting information that will help them make money. The students sat up and took notice when I announced that my first seminar was entitled "How to Lose Money" and that there would be no charge!

"There are three ways to lose money," I began. Then I explained that the first way is to neglect it. Money that's not invested wisely is money lost. I told them that I had in my possession some money from another country, which at the time of issue was worth US$37,000. However, by the time a friend gave it to me, it wasn't worth two cents. That means that if someone had put that amount under the mattress and taken it out seven years later, the currency would have been worthless.

The second way to lose money, I explained, is to abandon it. You remember the old saying "Finders keepers, losers weepers." Money must be protected or it will be lost. The teens were listening intently.

The third way to lose money, I pointed out, is simply to waste it—throw it away. When we lived in Southern Asia, I watched a wedding procession passing along the street. Someone in the wedding party was throwing coins to the onlookers. That's a sure way to lose money.

"My seminar on losing money is over," I announced. "How was it?"

No one was sleeping. This was fun. This guy with white hair wasn't so bad after all. I told them that my next seminar was going to be about how to lose your special friend—girlfriend or boyfriend. I continued to hold their attention. Then I proceeded to make clear that losing a girlfriend or boyfriend, or for that matter a husband or wife, is similar to what you do to lose money.

First, you can simply neglect them; second, you can abandon them; third, you can be unfaithful to them. What could be clearer? After explaining the main points for five or 10 minutes, I announced that my "How to Lose Your Special Friend" seminar was over and that I had one more seminar to present. It was "How to Lose Jesus as Your Friend."

The reader can guess the points in that seminar. The way to lose Jesus as a friend is the same as how to lose money or lose someone you really care about. The chapel period was over, and I felt good about what I'd done. The young people were all smiles. I'd hit a home run.

The Week of Prayer devotionals also went well, I felt. On Friday someone from the Youth Sabbath school called and asked if I'd talk to the class the next day. *Oh no,* I thought to myself. *What will I do now?* But I couldn't say no, so I decided to wing it the best I could.

It came my time to speak. "We're glad that Pastor O'Ffill is with us this morning, and he'll talk to us now."

I stood up. "Do you remember me?"

"Yes, we remember you," they said. "You spoke to us at chapel on Monday."

"Do you remember what I talked about?"

"Yes, you told us how to lose money."

I could hardly believe it. I hadn't just hit a home run—I'd hit a grand slam. I asked them if they remembered how to lose money. They immediately told me that we lose money by neglecting it, abandoning it, or wasting it.

"What else did I talk about?"

"You told us how to lose our girlfriend or boyfriend."

When I asked how, they immediately said, "You lose your girlfriend or boyfriend the same way you lose your money." I was on the verge of signing up to be a youth pastor! Then I asked, "What else did I talk about?"

Silence.

"Come on now," I cajoled. "That was the main point."

More silence. Then someone ventured, "We don't remember."

The point of that experience was not lost on me. When I talked about money and girlfriends/boyfriends, I was answering questions they had. Losing Jesus as a friend wasn't a problem they were aware of at the time.

What we see as our children's problems and what they perceive as their problems may not necessarily be the same. It's easy to understand how difficult it can be for parents to communicate with children if we aren't on the same wavelength.

Contemporary society does not have "How to Lose Jesus as a Friend" very high on its list of concerns. How to be rich, sexy, powerful, and how to feel good about yourself are the engines that drive today's culture, and our children are being carried along by these currents.

Traditional standards of right and wrong have become passé in the modern culture. Parents and their children often live in two separate worlds with respect to standards of behavior. Even among the young generation who still go to church it's noticeable that what is deemed as acceptable Sabbath observance may be decidedly different from their parents' concepts.

Inasmuch as parents are seen by their children as authority figures, even after they are adults, and inasmuch as God is the ultimate authority, it's often difficult for our children to have an objective conversation with us about spiritual matters. When our children are having a spiritual crisis, we should not be surprised if this spills over into their relationship with us, inasmuch as they may see us as God's representatives in their lives.

Men are problem solvers. When someone shares a problem with us, our assumption is that they want us to solve it. Of course, this is not necessarily the case. It's probably more accurate to recognize that when someone shares a problem, what they really are looking for is someone who agrees with what they have already decided—or maybe they just want a listening ear as they vent.

As I've mentioned previously in this book, I'm not naturally a good listener, especially where members of the family are involved. My tendency is to want them to get to the point so that I can tell them what I think about the matter. One of the biggest challenges I have in relating to our grown children is learning how to be a good listener. Because we have an emotional conflict of interest for the simple reason that they are our children, it's difficult to listen dispassionately.

Two psychiatrists worked in the same office building. One was just beginning his practice, and the other apparently had been plying his trade for many years. They rode up on the same elevator each morning and by chance usually rode down together at the end of the day.

In the morning they were both fresh and fit as they rode up to their respective suites, but at the end of the day it was another matter. The older doctor still appeared fresh and chipper even after a full day, whereas the younger looked haggard and utterly exhausted.

Finally the younger of the two could resist no longer. Riding together one day after work, he asked his colleague, "How do you manage to spend hours listening to all the garbage your patients tell you and still look so fresh and rested at the end of the day?"

The man with experience replied, "Who listens?"

When our children share their problems, we must learn to listen calmly without becoming upset. But this isn't easy to do, because we love them and care for them so much.

It took me a long time to notice that when my son came to talk with me and I immediately gave my opinion on things, he would have no more to say. I had to learn what is called reflective listening, in which I rephrased what he'd been saying without putting in my own two cents' worth. This would seem to encourage him, and he would continue with what he was trying to say.

After having been the children's problem solver for so many years, I haven't found it easy to realize that those days are over. I now have a new role to play, that of being a listening, caring parent who thinks he knows what they need in order to solve their problems but is finally getting smart enough not to say it—then.

Parents are loaded with advice and like to share it liberally. However, even though we have something the children need—experience—we should try to share it on a by-request basis. I may be dreaming, but perhaps if we learn to do this, the time might actually come when our grown children ask, "Dad, what do you think I should do?"

Then, when I've picked myself up off the floor, I will tell them!

However, people persuaded against their will are of the same opinions still. So I should not be terribly surprised if they listen but do something different. What should we do when we can't solve the problem? We can at least listen. Even if we say nothing, all is not lost. If they are given the opportunity to explain their feelings and we are doing reflective listening, it can help them better understand the issues involved, and in the end they solve their own problem.

One day I was talking with my uncle who is a psychiatrist. I told him I'd been talking with someone, and the person had given me a certain insight. My uncle pointed out that we don't give people insights. An insight is something that comes from inside ourselves. I'd never thought of it that way before, but now I understand that what we learn from someone else won't become useful until we make it part of ourselves.

Ultimately, no one can solve a problem for someone else. We can help in solving the problem, but people own their problems and so must solve them themselves. Parents can pray that they might be able to say or do something that will encourage their children to solve their problems in a way that is in harmony with God's will.

CONSIDER THESE THINGS

1. People don't hear us when we answer questions they are not asking.
2. Most people don't want us to solve their problems; they want someone to talk to.
3. When we do look for counsel, we tend to try to find someone who reflects our point of view.
4. If someone asks you for your advice, don't be surprised if he or she does something else.
5. Insights come from inside.

DISCUSS WITH SOMEONE

1. Practice with each other the art of reflective listening.
2. Discuss how we can listen without getting emotionally involved. (Hint: We must think of the other person and not of ourselves.)

A PARENT'S PRAYER

Heavenly Father, You so often try to impress our hearts through the Holy Spirit, but we do not hear because we are thinking about something else. Thank You for not giving up on us, and for trying in every situation to get through to us. Help us, Lord, to learn to listen to others like You listen to us. When others talk to us, we often listen with the focus of how what they are saying will impact us. We want to learn to think of the needs of others instead. It is our desire that the Holy Spirit will do whatever it takes to make us as truly caring for others as Jesus is for us. Amen.

THIRTEEN

IF I HAD IT TO DO AGAIN

"Making mistakes simply means you are learning faster."—Weston H. Agor.

In a previous chapter I mentioned that I worked for a plastering contractor when I was a student. I began as the one who mixed and carried the plaster. Later I was given the opportunity to actually apply the material to the wall.

One day we were applying the finish coat. One of the experienced men noticed what I was doing and said, "That's not the way to do it." He then proceeded to show me the way it was supposed to be done.

I watched him for a while and said, "But you don't do it that way yourself."

Then he said something that has been helpful through the years. "Learn how it's supposed to be done, and then do it any way you want."

Many parents are raising children any way they want without knowing how it's supposed to be done. As a result, a lot of improvising and trial and error go on. Although we can study how to be parents, when our baby arrives it isn't a simulation. It's the real thing!

In the chapters of this book I've encouraged a lot of looking back. I defend this because in the first place it helps us know where we have come from, and in the second place it shows us where we are going unless we make some midcourse corrections.

Sometimes a couple will raise a family, and then a number of years later another child is born. It's often referred to as "our surprise" or "our bonus baby." When this happens, it's almost like raising two separate families. Betty and I had our four children within the space of nine years. Then when we were in our 50s another child came into our lives in a way we couldn't have imagined.

When Andrea was born, I was her grandpa before I was her mother's father-in-law. Because they had no other place to go, we took the young couple into our home. The marriage lasted barely two years, so the wife and the baby went home to her mother. But at that stage of her life she didn't feel able to raise the child, so one day our son brought the baby back to our home. And so began for us an experience that lasted for the next five years.

When people tell you they raised a grandchild, you can be sure there's a sad story between the lines. In our case there certainly was. But I'll thank God forever that He gave me an opportunity to go around again. If I had my life to live over again, would I live it differently? Yes, of course. Maybe not in its broadest outlines but surely in many of its details.

If I were to tell you in what ways raising a granddaughter differed from raising my own children, I'd explain that the second time around I was more *kind*. Not that I was necessarily unkind with our own children, but the second time around I really worked at it.

When you're a young father, one of the points you try to get across to the children is that you're the boss. To do this, you feel you have to throw your weight around, and nothing shows who's the boss like saying no. When my children would ask for a favor, I would often answer no. Not that I wouldn't eventually say yes, but starting off with a no definitely showed who was in charge. Or so I thought.

When I said no, the child making the request would say something like "Oh, please, Daddy. Let me do it." Wanting to reinforce my place as leader, I would say no a second time. This would result in the one making the request raising his or her voice and maybe even starting to cry. Then, having established my leadership, I'd begin to negotiate. With the child upset now, thoroughly upset, I'd reluctantly say yes. (I am, of course, exaggerating this illustration.)

But the second time around I realized that a person who's really in charge could say yes as easily as saying no and still be the boss. In fact, it was actually easier. So when Andrea would ask, "Grandpa, can I do . . . ," I'd stop what I was doing and listen. If what she was requesting was reasonable, even though it might inconvenience me a bit, I'd say yes. By now you're probably thinking that I'm the classic case of a grandparent spoiling the grandchild. I might have been tempted to spoil her if she'd been visiting us on holidays, but she lived with us for five years.

I wish I had caught on to this administrative tack the first time around, because I discovered that when I said no to my granddaughter, which occasionally I did, she didn't scream, cry, or otherwise make a scene. She'd simply drop the subject and go on to something else. When she'd turn and walk away peacefully, I wanted to ask, "But aren't you going to scream or beg?"

It's only now that I understand why she didn't carry on when I said no. With the first family I was at times not predictable, so a good cry and begging were necessary to find out if I might change my mind. But the second time around, something had changed—and it was I.

Another thing I learned the second time around was not

to label the child. If you ask your son or daughter to make the bed and they do it only once in a while, telling them they are lazy doesn't improve the situation. You see, not making one's bed is one thing, but calling them lazy is something quite different. It can easily turn into a self-fulfilling prophecy for the child. If young people haven't done the assigned homework because they were playing outside, it's one thing to insist that they must do their homework at the appropriate time, but it's quite another to call them dumb. Not doing homework is about the task. Calling someone dumb is about the person. We must be sensitive not to label each other. (We as spouses must be careful that we don't do this to each other either.)

During the years we had her, I tried to treat Andrea as a guest. It's said that good hospitality is when we treat someone like a member of the family. In too many homes this wouldn't be safe treatment! It would be a better idea to treat members of the family as guests.

Do we have to be older in order to be wiser? Some people are older and never got wiser along the way. But experience can be the best teacher, even if it is someone else's experience. I learned some practical things about raising children when I got a second chance.

Sometimes my granddaughter would come to where I was and say, "Grandpa, please help me make my bed."

In earlier years I would have likely said, "You know how to make your bed. Now go do it."

What I failed to realize back then was that when you're 5 years old, the bed comes up to your chest. Even the best of us discovers that sometimes the bed gets really messed up, and we need to make it all over again from scratch. When you're 5 years old, this can be a major undertaking.

When she pleaded, "Grandpa, help me make my bed,"

she wasn't trying to get out of work but, rather, was saying she had a problem that required two people to resolve. Therefore I'd go with her, and together we'd make the bed.

On other occasions she'd ask for help cleaning her room. This used to be a signal for me to give a speech on neatness. But through the years you learn that it's possible for a room to get so cluttered that even an adult doesn't know where to begin to straighten it up. So when my granddaughter would ask me to help clean her room, I interpreted this as a distress call, and together we cleaned the room.

How thankful I am that I was given this opportunity to take a practical graduate course in raising children. I may have received only passing grades the first time around, but through the grief and pain of the circumstances, it was the experience of the second time that has meant so much to me.

We sing in a little chorus that God is so good. Through the various stages of my life, God has been good to me—good in that although I make many mistakes, He does not put me down and call me names. That is what the text in James means: "If any of you lack wisdom, let him ask of God, that giveth to all men liberally, and *upbraideth not;* and it shall be given him" (James 1:5).

"Upbraideth not" means that He doesn't keep throwing things up to us as we so often do to each other. We can make the same mistake again and again, and He remains the same. Every time we desire from the heart to get it right, it is as if He says, "OK, let's try that again."

Hundreds of texts tell us what God is like. Here is one of my favorites: "And the Lord passed by before him, and proclaimed, The Lord, The Lord God, merciful and gracious, long-suffering, and abundant in goodness and truth" (Ex. 34:6).

If I had it to do all over again, that's the way I'd want to be—merciful, gracious, longsuffering, and abundant in goodness and truth. That's the way God is. It makes me feel good to ask Him to make me like that, too. After all, He is my heavenly Father, and He made it possible for me to be a father, and that's the kind of dad and granddad I want to be.

I know I still have a long way to go, but I think I'm making progress. We go to school not to discover what we already know but to discover what we don't know and to learn how to do it right. I might have been a drill sergeant dad the first time around, but that doesn't mean it's too late for me to make some late course corrections.

When we take an examination, we want to make a good grade, but only if we deserve it. When I was in the seminary, I had a teacher named Edward Heppenstall. I don't remember what course I was taking at the time; I only remember it had no quizzes, and the final test had only one question.

When Heppenstall returned to me the "blue book" in which I had written the exam, I noticed a big D scrawled across the first page and a note. It said, "Dick, what's wrong? Please come and see me."

In graduate school a grade of C is like an F, and so a D is even worse. I wasn't well-acquainted with the professor, but at the appointed time I approached him.

"What happened?" he asked again. "Didn't you understand the question?"

I told him that I hadn't at the time but that I now did. I could hardly believe it when he offered, "Write it again."

Three or four days later the rewritten exam came back. Across the top was a big B. I've never forgotten what that professor did for me. Years later when I taught Bible to academy students, I was able to return the favor by telling young scholars who'd done poorly in an exam that if they wished, they could write it again.

How thankful we can be that we have a heavenly Father

who says, "Write it again." Sometimes when I'm praying and confessing that I didn't do as well as I would have liked on the road through life, I say to Jesus, "Please, Lord, let me do that again."

When Jesus was on this earth, several times the heavenly Father announced, "This is my beloved Son, in whom I am well pleased." I want Him to be able to say about me that He is well pleased with me, one of His sons in the twenty-first century. I realize I don't hit a home run every time I come up to the plate. I still hit foul balls, and sometimes I even strike out. But by His grace I'm still in the game.

Betty and I got a second time around. We were broken-hearted about the circumstances which surrounded that opportunity, but the need was there, and we spent five years as parents again. Our granddaughter has now gone to live with her mother. But we believe we left our mark on her heart, and we know she left hers on ours.

CONSIDER THESE THINGS

1. God allows sad experiences because He knows they can draw us nearer to Him—if we will.
2. A boss doesn't have to be bossy!
3. We must resist the temptation to call each other names, because names can be who we are or who we will become.
4. In some cases it would be better to treat our family members as guests rather than to treat our guests as family members.
5. God doesn't throw our past in our face, and we shouldn't do that with each other either.

DISCUSS WITH SOMEONE

1. What would your home be like if you always made an effort to be kind?
2. What are some obvious things we can do to make our family members happier?

A PARENT'S PRAYER

Heavenly Father, thank You for sending the Holy Spirit to convict us of our mistakes. Oh, how much we want to be like You! You are so kind and loving. You don't call us names, and even when we make mistakes again and again, You don't fling it in our teeth. And when we are sorry from our hearts, You give us another chance. Please forgive us for the way we sometimes treat those we love. Lord, we are sorry to say that sometimes we treat total strangers better than we treat the people we love. Please don't give up on us. Do whatever it takes to remind us, and when we cry out for help, we know that You are always there to work in our lives. Thank You in Jesus' name, amen.

FOURTEEN

How to Be Involved
Without Getting Involved

"Teach us to care and not to care. Teach us to sit still."
—T. S. Eliot.

It was Sunday morning. My wife and I were enjoying our ritual of having a late breakfast and reading the paper. Betty pointed out an ad which announced that Wards was having a furniture sale. She called my attention to a kitchen table set in white and natural wood, with white tile set in the top. It had been 15 years since we'd bought our current set, and it was beginning to show wear and tear. The store opened at noon, so we decided that in the afternoon we'd go and check it out.

It was nearly 3:30 p.m. when we finally put Andrea in the car seat. I sat in the back, and Betty drove with Andrea at her side. (That was before children had to be riding in the back seat.) As we pulled out of the driveway Betty suggested that inasmuch as we were going to Wards, we might as well stop at a couple of other furniture stores on the way.

It's a known fact that generally men don't like to shop. I'd liked what had been advertised in the paper and could see no reason we shouldn't just go and buy the set. Besides, we were leaving late, and the store might close while we were still looking, and I didn't particularly want to spend a whole week shopping for a kitchen table! Nevertheless, I prepared myself to do some comparative shopping.

At our first stop they had the same basic style of table we'd seen in the paper, so I suggested we buy that one. Betty said we should go on down to Wards and see what they had. After having seen the set that was advertised, I must confess I liked the one at the first store and suggested we go back and buy it.

Women are good at shopping. Betty said that before we made up our minds, we should see what a third place had to offer. By now I was beginning to get nervous. Time was running out, and it wouldn't be long before the stores would close, and shopping for a kitchen table would have to be carried over to another day.

To make matters worse, we encountered a lot of traffic that Sunday. When we pulled out of Wards, we had to turn and go back the way we had come, which meant having to wait at a traffic light that seemed never to change. By now I just knew we were going to miss out on being able to finish this project. When the light finally changed, the traffic didn't move at once, so I said to Betty, "Honk the horn."

She replied quietly, "I can't. I'm not a type A personality."

She might as well have slapped me in the face! We hadn't been discussing personality types, and here she was accusing me of being a type A personality. I could feel anger welling up from the pit of my stomach. I just couldn't let her get away with insulting me this way. I wanted to say something that would even the score.

Traffic was moving by now, and as we drove along I said nothing, although I was upset. I was trying to think of something to say that would let her know I didn't appreciate what she'd expressed. Then my conscience began to talk to me: *Is it true? Are you a type A personality?*

Well, I thought to myself, *I suppose if you want to put it that way, yes, I guess I am.*

Then it was as if my conscience said to me, *If it's true, then why are you upset?*

I began to do some serious thinking. I realized I often pray that God will show me where I need to change. I guess I'd never thought about how He'd go about it. Had I assumed that I'd have dreams and visions or that a voice from heaven would speak to me? Or would an animal speak to me as it did to Balaam? It never occurred to me that God might use my wife to say something I needed to hear.

By now I wasn't angry anymore. Betty had meant nothing by what she'd said, and she wasn't even aware of the battle that had gone on in my heart. I learned something very important that day. Whenever someone apparently puts me down, before I get upset I would do well to ask myself the question Is it true? And if it is, then I should thank God that He is trying to get through to me any way He can. By the way, we bought the kitchen set from the last store. It was by far the prettiest!

Valentine's Day was approaching, and I felt the urge to do something special for Betty that year, so I asked her what she thought about going out to eat. By nature we men aren't always very spontaneous, so I considered this a wonderfully romantic gesture! It was like asking a girl out for a date, but this time the girl was my wife.

I wasn't prepared for her response: "Why don't we just exchange cards this year?"

Now, it's hard on a man's ego to be turned down when he's asking a girl out for a date, and I'd just been turned down. The worst part was that this was my wife. Now I was angry. This really hurt me. Betty had rebuffed my attempt to do something special for her on, of all days, Valentine's Day.

My immediate reaction was that I needed to teach her a lesson. So I decided that inasmuch as she'd suggested only exchanging cards, I'd go one better and give her nothing. Then when she wondered why, it would be my chance to tell her how I felt about having been turned down when I'd asked her out for a date. If you had seen me, you would never have known what I was plotting. I didn't say or do anything at the time that would give her any idea of how angry and insulted I felt.

A day or two passed. I still felt angry and figured I needed to teach her a lesson. But now it occurred to me that instead of not giving her anything, perhaps the best way to make my point would be to give her some flowers. I'd show her up! To me that seemed like a better plan, so when the day finally arrived, I went to a flower shop and purchased an arrangement that would fit on her desk at work.

But I didn't want to hand-deliver the flowers. Although what I was doing appeared to be romantic, it really wasn't. I decided to leave them with the receptionist, and she could call Betty and tell her someone had left her something at the reception desk. The receptionist was all smiles and must have wished that her husband were as romantic as I. She told me, however, that Betty was not in her office but had gone across the street to my office.

Fortunately our paths didn't cross as I returned to my building. But when I entered my office, I was shocked to find on my desk a package and a love note. I'm embarrassed to say that not only did I receive one package and a love note that Valentine's Day, but eventually I received at least three other packages and three other love notes. The stinger was stung!

I'm glad that at least I bought her flowers, although I felt ashamed of the things that had gone through my mind. Later when I related to her what had really happened, she was surprised and told me that when she'd suggested we exchange cards it was only because she didn't want to be a bother.

It's difficult to be involved without getting involved. This is usually because we have our own self-interests, and sometimes we consider what is going on as a direct insult or offense against us personally. When our children have their problems, it's easy for us to become part of the problem.

How can we be involved in our children's lives without becoming part of the problem? This book has sought to emphasize the importance of parents keeping their own hearts and homes in order even while the children's lives may be unstable and unpredictable. Parents must ask God to help both themselves and their children to be both stable and predictable.

Our family is fortunate that through all we have experienced, our own parents (the children's grandparents), though grieved, were not shaken. They seemed to be able to see things in the long term, and when we feared that our world was coming to an end, Grandma would say, "It's going to be all right," then, mentioning the child by name, would add that Jesus loved them and they were going to be all right too.

How can we be involved without getting directly involved?

1. Understand the importance of being stable and predictable. We must at times bite our lip and just be there. We can be like the ballast in a boat that keeps it from tipping in a great storm.

2. Understand that although there may appear to be a change of loyalty, the children still love us and appreciate us, though perhaps not in the same way they did before. There are more players and more issues in their lives now. We used to be everything, but now we're just a part, howbeit an important part.

3. We must resist the temptation to threaten them with consequences. Secretly we may wish they could be taught a lesson, and we sometimes unconsciously communicate this by our attitudes. They can sense this and are not comfortable being with us.

4. We must not let the circumstances of their lives control the agenda of ours. If this happens, we will not be able to give them the help they need.

5. We should not maximize, but minimize, our input.

6. Sometimes we will find we're like the fire department or the ambulance. We aren't called until an emergency arises. The challenge then is to respond appropriately without saying "I told you so" or feeling we're being used.

7. If we get involved in the wrong ways, we can find ourselves actually enabling the problem. Doing nothing or doing the wrong thing can prolong the problem and even make it worse.

8. We must pray that the Lord will give us a spirit of compassion. We know what compassion is. We experienced it when they were young and had a bad case of chicken pox.

9. We should remember the golden rule. If we were in their place, what would we want our parents to do for us?

10. Even when things are at their worst, our task is to give hope.

Experience is the greatest of teachers. Some people learn from the experiences of others, while some must get experience for themselves. Who will do which, and why, is a mystery.

Like it or not, we're involved in the lives of our children. We can wash our hands and say we aren't, but we are nevertheless. The question isn't if we will be involved, but how we will be involved. Will our input add to their problem? Will it be like a lighthouse that, although unable to take a ship out of the storm, keeps it from breaking up on the rocks?

CONSIDER THESE THINGS

1. Look for times when God is trying to tell you something about yourself.

2. Those who know us best are the ones who live with us.
3. Broken homes can happen as a result of a misunderstanding.
4. The Bible says that we are never to repay evil for evil, whether real or perceived (Rom. 12:19-21).
5. "A soft answer turneth away wrath: but grievous words stir up anger" (Prov. 15:1).

DISCUSS WITH SOMEONE

1. What are some of the things we can do that won't make it worse when we feel we've been insulted?
2. What are some of the correct ways we can be involved in our children's lives?

A PARENT'S PRAYER

Our Father, who is in heaven, so much of what we are going through is new to us. We have never been this way before, and sometimes we don't know what to do or say. Our children sometimes appear to want us to be involved in their lives, but when we are, they get upset.

Lord, we need to know from experience what David meant when he said: "Great peace have they which love thy law: and nothing shall offend them" (Ps. 119:165). We are offended so easily, and we also find ourselves at times offending others, especially those we love so much. One thing is sure; with Your help and strength we are going to stay with You and learn what we need so that we can be the kind of parents and grandparents You can use to save our families. In Jesus' name, amen.

FIFTEEN

NEVER GIVE UP

"Success doesn't mean the absence of failures; it means the attainment of ultimate objectives. It means winning the war, not every battle."—Edward Bliss.

Until now I'd never really understood the importance of the two words "patience" and "hope." Perhaps I never learned to be patient because I wasn't forced to, and hope wasn't important because my future was always now. In this generation the modus operandi has been if you want it, get it. This perspective has affected not only our ability to save for something we want to buy but also our ability to wait for things that are sacred and based on commitment.

In my childhood Christmas and summer required patience and hope. Christmas was special because, as children, we got things on Christmas we couldn't have during the rest of the year. And summer was special because we could eat strawberries, fresh tomatoes, and corn on the cob. Nowadays it isn't necessary to wait either for Christmas or for summer. If I want something, I simply go out and buy it. And as far as strawberries, tomatoes, and corn on the cob go, they're available all the time at my local supermarket.

This generation doesn't like to wait because it hasn't had to wait. They haven't had to learn patience. We're faced with the fact that our children often do not seem to be interested in spiritual things. They marry out of the church and set up a lifestyle that has little to do with the one they were raised in.

We went into debt to give them a Christian education, and it appears to be all for nothing.

We pray that the Lord will save them, but for the time being, nothing seems to be changing. Another divorce; another marriage. We begin to wonder if it will ever end. Other parents tell their success stories. We can't say much, but we often question if our prayers are doing any good.

The situation can be intensified by the proximity of the loved ones. When they're in our house or in the same town, it can be an everyday challenge that keeps us continually drained. Sometimes we wish we could take a break and get on with our own lives for a while. At this stage we'd thought things would be getting a little better as far as the family is concerned, but with the passing years life can become more complicated than ever.

The Bible is like a pharmacy. You may not need everything on the shelves at the same time, but you can never come to the place without there being just what you need. I hadn't noticed it before, probably because I didn't need it like I do now, but suddenly the call of Scripture to be patient is extremely relevant in my life. I've found some wonderful texts that highlight the importance of patience.

"Better is the end of a thing than the beginning thereof: and the patient in spirit is better than the proud in spirit" (Eccl. 7:8).

"To them who by patient continuance in well doing seek for glory and honour and immortality, eternal life" (Rom. 2:7).

"Rejoicing in hope; patient in tribulation; continuing instant in prayer" (Rom. 12:12).

"Be patient therefore, brethren, unto the coming of the Lord. Behold, the husbandman waiteth for the precious fruit of the earth, and hath long patience for it, until he receive the early and latter rain" (James 5:7).

"Be ye also patient; stablish your hearts: for the coming of the Lord draweth nigh" (James 5:8).

My heart is touched because these texts seem to describe the struggles and concerns we all have for our children and grandchildren. I don't have a difficult time putting myself in the following texts.

"And not only so, but we glory in tribulations also: knowing that tribulation worketh patience; and patience, experience; and experience, hope" (Rom. 5:3, 4).

"But if we hope for that we see not, then do we with patience wait for it" (Rom. 8:25).

"For whatsoever things were written aforetime were written for our learning, that we through patience and comfort of the scriptures might have hope" (Rom. 15:4).

"But in all things approving ourselves as the ministers of God, in much patience, in afflictions, in necessities, in distresses" (2 Cor. 6:4).

"Strengthened with all might, according to his glorious power, unto all patience and longsuffering with joyfulness" (Col. 1:11).

"Remembering without ceasing your work of faith, and labour of love, and patience of hope in our Lord Jesus Christ, in the sight of God and our Father" (1 Thess. 1:3).

"So that we ourselves glory in you in the churches of God for your patience and faith in all your persecutions and tribulations that ye endure" (2 Thess. 1:4).

"For ye have need of patience, that, after ye have done the will of God, ye might receive the promise" (Heb. 10:36).

"Wherefore seeing we also are compassed about with so great a cloud of witnesses, let us lay aside every weight, and the sin which doth so easily beset us, and let us run with patience the race that is set before us" (Heb. 12:1).

"Knowing this, that the trying of your faith worketh patience. But let patience have her perfect work, that ye may be perfect and entire, wanting nothing" (James 1:3, 4).

As I read these texts, I notice the link between patience, tribulation, and suffering. When we pray from the heart that God will develop in us the fruit of the Spirit, we must understand that suffering is the price we'll have to pay. It is from suffering and trials that character is developed. Most of us resist the idea of suffering. We conclude that if we do things correctly and if we're the right kind of people, we won't have to suffer. The texts just cited indicate that this is not the case. Trials, suffering, and tribulation are what living in this world, especially as Christians, is all about.

Patience is an *enabling gift* because it gives us the quality to wait for the Lord while He works in us both to will and to do His good pleasure. It is the gift that enables us to endure suffering. When we're faced with trouble, the number one issue is if we'll take matters into our own hands or if we'll trust the Lord. Here's where there is a fundamental conflict, because we want our problems solved now.

I'm told that some mushrooms mature in 24 hours, whereas a tree may take a generation to reach maturity. We must remind ourselves when we become weary that raising children isn't something we do in 24 hours but rather something that happens over a lifetime.

This generation isn't into life with a view toward the long haul. What we do, we think we must do quickly, and this affects our ability to deal with things that have long-term importance. One of the greatest tragedies of our age is the broken home. Often people seem to have more reasons for not staying married than for staying married. I was conducting a weekend revival at a church, and the matter of living with non-Christian spouses came up. Two widows shared their experiences. Both had been married to nonbelievers. In both cases the lives of the women during more than 40 years of marriage had been difficult and not without a share of grief. Yet the women had stayed with their husbands and continued to pray.

One related how after 40 years her husband gave his life to Jesus and said to his wife, "Thank you for not giving up on me." The experience of the other widow was similar.

I was attending a training workshop for lay pastors when a man whom I didn't remember having met before walked up to me. He asked who I was, and I told him. Tears welled up in his eyes as he said, "Pastor O'Ffill, the last time I saw you, you were conducting my mother's funeral. I was there, half drunk."

Years before, his mother had been my secretary and had died of Lou Gehrig's disease. All her life she'd prayed for this son. Had I asked her on her deathbed about her son, she would have told me that he was still an alcoholic. Had I asked her if God had answered her prayer for her boy, she would have answered no. Bill and I embraced and thanked God for a mother's prayers.

It's hard to accept the fact that we might not live to see our prayers answered. Sometimes I feel I can't look anymore. Sometimes I wonder if God hears. Sometimes I need more patience.

Whereas patience gives us the strength to bear the present, hope takes us from the present to a joyful tomorrow. I've come to the conclusion that hope is the alternative to giving up. Hope is more than just wishful thinking. A tongue-in-cheek saying is "I feel so much better now that I've given up hope!" That isn't the hope God offers.

We need to wrestle with how to relate the reality of the present with the hope for the future. At times we're tempted to think from what we see now that all is lost. Sometimes we feel it might be easier to resign oneself to reality as we see it.

Accept the unacceptable and consider the battle lost. But this is where hope steps in and stops our emotional free fall.

Hope isn't based on what we can see. It's not based on the five senses. Hope is putting our faith in the invisible and centering our emotional focus on something that hasn't happened yet. The Bible tells us how hope works.

"For we are saved by hope: but hope that is seen is not hope: for what a man seeth, why doth he yet hope for?" (Rom. 8:24).

"But if we hope for that we see not, then do we with patience wait for it" (Rom. 8:25).

"Rejoicing in hope; patient in tribulation; continuing instant in prayer" (Rom. 12:12).

"For whatsoever things were written aforetime were written for our learning, that we through patience and comfort of the scriptures might have hope" (Rom. 15:4).

"Now the God of hope fill you with all joy and peace in believing, that ye may abound in hope, through the power of the Holy Ghost" (Rom. 15:13).

"Or saith he it altogether for our sakes? For our sakes, no doubt, this is written: that he that ploweth should plow in hope; and that he that thresheth in hope should be partaker of his hope"(1 Cor. 9:10).

The hope spoken of in these texts is not the hope the world offers. Hinduism teaches that we create our own reality in our minds; whatever we think, is. However, the Christian's hope is based not on a fantasy created in the mind, but rather on the promises of the real and living God.

Patience is about the present, and hope is about the future. When we have prayed for patience, then next we must pray for hope. Please note the following:

1. For our part we are to have hope. Hope is something God gives us that is coupled to faith. Hope enables us to look beyond the present and see a new beginning. But here we

must limit ourselves to what God has revealed in His Word. The future has been promised but not in all its detail. However, enough has been revealed so that we may understand that the sad reality of today will not be the joyful reality of tomorrow until God wipes away all tears from our eyes and makes all things new.

2. We must not try to play God or do what only God can do. We tend to try to kick-start God. We think we know what needs to be done and how to do it. However, we must not get ahead of God. We're to be patient and to hope. This will necessitate putting our trust in Him and not in ourselves. In plain language, we must resist taking matters into our own hands.

Being patient and having hope isn't easy. We can become tired of being patient and having hope, but this is our part. "Without faith it is impossible to please him: for he that cometh to God must believe that he is, and that he is a rewarder of them that diligently seek him" (Heb. 11:6). Whether we live to see our prayers answered or, as in the case of my former secretary, meet our loved ones in the resurrection, we must never give up hope.

CONSIDER THESE THINGS

1. This generation is impatient. The result is people intent on instant gratification.
2. Scripture teaches that patience enables us to endure trouble.
3. Hope is the knowledge that the conditions of the present are not permanent.
4. We may not live to see our prayers for our children answered.
5. Patience and hope come to us as gifts, but we must ask for them and persist in them.

DISCUSS WITH SOMEONE

1. How will we know when God is giving us patience? What difference will it make in our outlook?
2. How can we harmonize the reality of the present with the hope for the future?

A PARENT'S PRAYER

Heavenly Father, we too often ask You to give us patience now. But, Lord, how can we endure the trials and sufferings of this life unless You give us this wonderful gift? You have promised that we will not be tried more than we can bear, and we know this is true. But Lord, please develop patience in our hearts so that we can wait for You as You work in our hearts and in the hearts of those we love.

Lord, You have promised us a new day when You will wipe away all tears from our eyes and everything that is painful will be gone forever. You have always fulfilled Your promises even when those who prayed didn't live to see it, but we know they will in the resurrection. Please forgive us for our lack of patience and hope. We try to push You into action, but You know what is best. Whatever it takes, we will learn to trust in You. We give You permission to—in Your way and in Your time—keep working in our lives and in the lives of those we love. Amen.

Sixteen

Lord, Teach Us to Pray

"Prayer does not change God, but changes him who prays."—Søren Kierkegaard.

Not many years ago a trip to an Adventist Book Center to find something on the subject of prayer would produce little more than the classic by Glenn Coon entitled *The ABC's of Bible Prayer.* Those lean days are over. Christian bookstores now have dedicated entire sections to prayer, and there are literally hundreds of titles.

Of all the elements of the Christian life, prayer is probably the spiritual discipline du jour. Some time ago I visited what is represented as an international prayer center located in Colorado Springs, Colorado. The impressive building houses a room of computers on which one may access live messages that are supposedly being sent by God through His messengers in various parts of the world.

Several years ago a group of "prayer warriors" was planning a trip to the ruins of the Ephesians' temple of Diana, where it planned to exorcise the demons that may yet be dwelling there. It's not uncommon to hear someone address the first part of the prayer to God and another part to the devil as they rebuke him, bind him, and cover him with the blood of Jesus.

Because our lives are increasingly complicated and the burdens we carry are so heavy, humanity desperately wants to find a solution. The word is out that prayer is power, and so we move toward prayer as a means of solving our problems.

In many places special prayer ministries are being organized, and those who participate are known as prayer warriors. These sincere people dedicate important amounts of time to prayer. Together with the act of prayer, attention is being given to fasting. In the city in which I live the leader of an international ministry is actively promoting 40 days of fasting each year. It is believed that God will surely answer our prayers if we fast. Churches eager to win their communities for Christ walk the streets in groups, claiming the ground for Christ.

In my own experience I've had the burden of prayer rest heavily upon my heart. I have studied prayer and have sat at the feet of men and women of prayer, trying desperately to learn how to pray in such a way that I could be sure God will answer my prayers.

One night a group of us were praying for a person who, the family believed, was being afflicted by demons. We'd begun to pray around 8:00 p.m., and now it was midnight. Still the young woman was making strange sounds. It seemed that our prayers were not doing any good. I remember thinking, *God, what are we doing wrong? Are You not answering our prayer because of a technicality?*

We live in an age of specialization. Is prayer now a victim of specialization? Does God answer only the prayers of the prayer warriors? In order to assure that our prayers for our children will be answered, must we say certain things in a certain way, and then only after we haven't eaten for several days?

When you hear miraculous stories of answered prayer, are you tempted to get in contact with such people because you conclude they must somehow have more influence with

God than you do and you want to ask them to please pray for you? The Bible says God is no respecter of persons (Acts 10:34). Is this true in everything except the matter of prayer?

In Luke 11:1 we read that when Jesus had finished praying in a certain place, one of the disciples came to Him and asked Him to teach them to pray. Jesus knew that this was a genuine request and gave the disciples, and all who would come after, the prayer on which all other prayers should be based.

The verses that follow the Lord's Prayer include an encouragement to pray and the assurance that God will hear and answer. Some have interpreted the promise in verses 5-13 to mean that if we say the right words and ask for good things, He will always give us what we're praying for. Practical experience, however, reveals otherwise. Even when we repeat words that seem right and ask for that which seems to be right, often nothing happens, or if it does, the result may not be what we'd hoped for.

We may come to believe that the reason for this disappointment is that we don't have enough faith. In the minds of many, faith seems to have taken on a life of its own. We assume that God will do whatever we ask, provided we exhibit enough faith. Is faith the secret to getting God to do what we ask? Often I have asked myself what faith is. I've come to the conclusion that faith is the belief that God can do what He has promised. Scripture relates that Jesus was unable to do miracles in many places because of the people's unbelief, lack of faith (Matt. 13:58). They still saw Him only as a carpenter's son from Nazareth.

Believing that our prayers are not answered because we lack faith can be especially painful when we're praying for God to save our children. When nothing seems to happen, we begin to believe it's because we're praying wrong. As a result, we begin to look at praying as a specific technique or a particular skill.

At a time when prayer seems to be the in thing and everyone is looking for the perfect way to pray, it's important to consider the following points:

1. Everyone is called to pray. Throughout history there have been men and women who have been mighty in prayer, but I cannot find that Scripture anywhere declares prayer an exclusive gift. The apostle Paul enumerates the gifts of the Spirit to the church in several places, including Ephesians 4:11, where he writes: "And he gave some, apostles; and some, prophets; and some, evangelists; and some, pastors and teachers." In 1 Corinthians 12 he adds other gifts, including faith, healing, miracles, prophecy, discerning of spirits, diverse tongues, interpretation of tongues, helping others, and government (see verses 9, 10, 28). Nowhere does he include prayer among the gifts.

While different members have different spiritual gifts, the *entire church* is called to pray. I point this out for the simple reason that we must not succumb to the idea that some people have the gift of prayer and others do not. I must not believe that God hears the prayers of others but not my own.

Although it is true that there are conditions for answered prayer, these conditions are universal and apply equally to everyone.

2. It is important that we do not see prayer as a type of magic. Prayer is neither magic nor a demand note, an IOU. The act of praying is more analogous to clearing away the underbrush that shuts out a view than to begging on the street. Prayer is sometimes seen as an attempt to control or channel divine power. It's not prayer that is powerful, but God who is powerful. Jesus said, "If ye have faith as a grain of mustard seed, ye shall say unto this mountain,

Remove hence to yonder place; and it shall remove; and nothing shall be impossible unto you" (Matt. 17:20).

The text may seem to be saying that if we have the right amount of faith we can do anything we want, but Jesus is really teaching us that if we'll put our trust in God, there's nothing He cannot do, even if it means having to move mountains. (In a practical sense, the mountains represent difficulties and challenges, not a chain of peaks such as the Colorado Rockies.)

Another oft-quoted text is "Delight thyself also in the Lord; and he shall give thee the desires of thine heart" (Ps. 37:4). The implication is that if I delight myself in the Lord, I can have anything I want. What is easily overlooked is that when we delight ourselves in the Lord, the desires of the heart are always to seek first the kingdom of God and His righteousness and to do the Lord's will, not our own.

The purpose of prayer is not to persuade God to do good things for us. After all, He is the giver of every good and perfect gift. "Every good gift and every perfect gift is from above, and cometh down from the Father of lights, with whom is no variableness, neither shadow of turning" (James 1:17). Neither is the purpose of prayer to convince God to do what we think needs to be done; rather, it is the process by which our hearts are brought into harmony with His. Only then are we are able to pray, "Not my will, but thine, be done" (Luke 22:42).

One popular faith healer is quoted as saying that when we pray we don't need to say, "If it be thy will." Instead, we should just tell God what we want Him to do. In reality nothing could be further from the truth.

3. *We must not tire of praying.* We usually have a certain expectation from prayer, namely, that God will give us what we're asking for and that He will do it soon, as in the oft quoted example: "Lord, give me patience, and give it to me *now.*" Because things don't seem to be turning out as we expect or as soon as we expect, we often risk the danger of growing tired of praying. Jesus warned us, "And he spake a parable unto them to this end, that men ought always to pray, and not to faint" (Luke 18:1).

The apostle Paul was short and to the point when he urged, "Pray without ceasing" (1 Thess. 5:17). He simply meant not to give up praying. When we stop praying, it means one of two things: either we've decided to accept the status quo, or we've decided to do it our way.

In the book *Transforming Prayer* I wrote that the purpose of prayer is not *to get* but *to be.* People who see prayer as the goose that lays the golden eggs will try every trick in the book to figure out just the places to be or the words to say that will produce the desired effects, and when the results are not forthcoming, they'll tend to reconfigure their prayers. If that doesn't work, they may give up praying altogether.

4. God knows all the pieces of the puzzle. We tend to pray about our most obvious needs. God is eager to do for us that which we may not even be aware needs to be done, and that which may be even more important than that for which we were praying. Scripture puts it this way: "Now unto him that is able to do exceeding abundantly above all that we ask or think, according to the power that worketh in us" (Eph. 3:20).

We read several stories in the Gospels in which Jesus disappointed the immediate expectations of those who were asking for help so that He could do more for them than they were aware needed to be done.

One day when Jesus was in the area of Tyre and Sidon, a Canaanite woman came to Him, asking Him to heal her daughter (Matt. 15:21-28). She had heard He could cast out demons, and so she was direct and to the point. "Have mercy on me, O Lord, thou son of David; my daughter is grievously vexed with a devil."

At first Jesus seemingly ignored her. When He finally acknowledged her, it was with apparently harsh words. The distraught mother, who had hoped for a miracle for her daughter, now found herself confronted with rudeness and racial slurs. But instead of being offended or becoming discouraged, she approached even closer and pleaded, "Lord, help me."

As a result, not only was her daughter healed, but she also discovered that praying to Jesus must be based on helpless dependency on Him no matter what the cost.

The story of Lazarus, whose family had an in with Jesus, offers another example. When Mary and Martha called on Jesus to come and heal their brother, they expected preferential treatment. When they didn't receive it, they later went so far as to chide Him: "Lord, if thou hadst been here, my brother had not died" (John 11:21, 32).

Had Jesus rushed to their side the moment they called, it would have been just another run-of-the-mill healing as far as the people were concerned. But the subsequent death and resurrection of Lazarus had a positive influence on many as well as entrenching the religious leaders in their desire to get rid of Jesus.

Though at times we may think God is being insensitive, by His very nature He always does what is for His glory and the advancement of His kingdom—and what is ultimately best for us. Even as we pray for our families, we must bear in mind that there's more involved in saving our children than simply our children. The great controversy between Christ and Satan rages on. This controversy and the rules that govern it take precedence. In mathematics the whole is the sum of its parts, but in the great war between good and evil, the parts can be saved only in the context of the whole.

The purpose of our prayers is not to change God's mind, but rather to give us an insight into His mind. He doesn't need to be reminded of who He is. It is we who need to be reminded. Prayer does not bend Him to us but us to Him. Put another way, the value of prayer is not that He will hear us . . . but that we will finally hear Him.

I've sometimes wondered what our attitude toward God would be if He gave us everything we wanted when we wanted it. Though this might seem to be a dream come true, we'd soon see Him as someone to be manipulated and appeased, which is exactly how pagans relate to their gods.

The purpose of prayer is not to solve our problems in this life but to prepare us for the life to come. Most of our prayers tend to be narrowly focused. Although we may pray for the right things, it may be for the wrong reasons. The prayer that is, in effect, trying to use God for whatever reason isn't true prayer.

You may have heard of the approach to prayer called "Name It and Claim It." Although God is no respecter of persons, it's difficult to conceive that what He has done for anyone at a particular time He will do for everyone all the time. This approach is not consistent with what prayer is meant to be, and can finally result in our creating gods who will serve us, when in reality we should be trying to discover the God we are meant to serve.

At a time when prayer may very well have been turned into a talisman, we are thankful for Christ's instructions: "And when thou prayest, thou shalt not be as the hypocrites are: for they love to pray standing in the synagogues and in the corners of the streets, that they may be seen of men. [Remember, prayer is not for the few but for all.] Verily I say unto you, They have their reward. But thou, when thou prayest, enter into thy closet, and when thou hast shut thy door [praying from the heart], pray to thy Father which is in secret; and thy Father which seeth in secret shall reward thee openly. But when ye pray, use not vain repetitions [prayer techniques], as the heathen do: for they think that they shall be heard for their much speaking. Be not ye therefore like unto them: for your Father knoweth what things ye have need of, before ye ask him. [What can we tell the omniscient One that we need that He doesn't already know?]" (Matt. 6:5-8).

In the end, our children will not be saved because we had the gift of prayer or because we had vast amounts of faith so that God was forced to change His mind and decided that He would save them. He calls on us to pray, not for His sake, but for ours. It's enough that we cry out as did the Canaanite woman, "Lord, help me!"

Do our prayers matter? Of course they do. God works on this planet as an answer to prayer. Our prayers for our children continually remind us that He ever lives to intercede for us (Heb. 7:25). Our prayers make us colaborers together with Him for the salvation of those we love. When Moses pleaded with God to give Israel another opportunity or blot his name out of the book of life, the appeal was not a test of God's love and commitment to save the lost but of Moses' self-sacrificing love for his people. And so it is with us as we pray, "God, keep Your mansions—just save my children."

CONSIDER THESE THINGS

1. It is not prayer that is powerful, but rather God who is powerful.
2. Faith is putting our confidence in God and not in ourselves.
3. God hears prayers at the level of the heart and not the lips.

4. Our prayers for others who are not praying for themselves act as a spiritual life-support system.
5. We should bring God our problems as we see them, but we should be careful about telling Him what to do about them.

DISCUSS WITH SOMEONE

1. How can we extend our prayer beyond the obvious need?
2. Why will we never lose if our prayers are based on the principle of "Thy kingdom come. Thy will be done"? What kinds of requests actually stand in the way of God answering them?

A PARENT'S PRAYER

Dear Father in heaven, just as the disciples came to Jesus and asked Him to teach them to pray, so we do that just now. We can see how we tend to use prayer to manipulate You and try to get You to do what we want. Please forgive us. The problems of this life are so overwhelming that we desperately try to solve them. How can we know how to pray unless You teach us?

Lord, please increase our faith. We have a difficult time trusting in You. We put our hand in Yours and then try to move Your hand around. We thank You that You are merciful and kind and don't hold our weaknesses against us.

You know how much we want our children to be saved. We love them so much, but we know You love them even more. They are Your children. When we pray for them, please don't look at us, but look into our hearts. Hear what we really mean, not how we express it. All we really mean is "Lord, help us!" Help us not to get tired or discouraged. You want to do more for us than we can imagine. We don't deserve it, but we give You thanks now and forever. Amen.

Seventeen

No Greater Love

"Surely it is not true blessedness to be free from sorrow while there is sorrow and sin in the world; sorrow is then a part of love, and love does not seek to throw it off."—George Eliot.

The phone in my office rang. It had now been 11 years since that New Year's Eve I sat weeping on the screened-in back porch. The voice on the phone was my son's. "Dad, I need help."

The previous evening one of my daughters had called and almost hysterically informed us that her brother was a drug addict. He had confided in her several weeks earlier and had promised, as so often happens, to quit, but he hadn't. He told her he was beginning to have problems with his heart. She was desperate. "He's going to hate me for telling you, but you must do something."

We weren't totally surprised. We suspected something wasn't right, and on at least one occasion I'd talked with his wife, and we'd cried and prayed together. Betty and I discussed what we should do, and we decided that the next day we'd confront him with what we knew and urge him to get treatment.

That morning even before the phone rang I'd been getting information about drug-treatment programs. I wasted no time. "I'll be right over," I said.

Only parents who have been through a similar experience can understand what words cannot express. As we drove together to the emergency room he took my hand and told me what a waste his life had been. I'll never forget the emotions. We both wept.

At the emergency room the attending physician, a Christian, was himself the father of a drug abuser. His son was at that moment in prison. He said it was probably for the best, because he knew the young man would be safer there than on the streets. Looking my boy in the eye, he said, "Son, there's no hope for you except with God. The only one who can change your life is Jesus."

What would parents do without Jesus!

There's a text that when first read may not sound right. But it must be right, because it records the words of Jesus Himself: "He that loveth father or mother more than me is not worthy of me: and he that loveth son or daughter more than me is not worthy of me" (Matt. 10:37).

Sometimes in desperation we're tempted to think that unless our loved ones are saved we don't want to go to heaven. This, of course, is an expression of our desperate love. But we must be careful that we don't unconsciously use ourselves as hostages for the salvation of our children. Scripture commands that we put first things first. We must love the Lord with all our heart, with all our soul, and with all our mind (Matt. 22:37). As the Holy Spirit implements this principle in our lives, our faith will increase, and our love for our children will become mature and stable.

God used us to create our children. We must not claim them as our own but as His. Just as Hannah raised her boy, Samuel, for the service of the Temple, so we will be comforted to know that, having done what we could, we now return—in our minds—our sons and daughters to the Lord.

Jesus said, "Greater love hath no man than this, that a man lay down his life for his friends" (John 15:13). Although we're still alive to tell about it, we have in so many ways laid down our lives for our children. From the time they were little ones, through their childhood, adolescence, and now with homes of their own, they continue to be in our thoughts and in our prayers.

Of all the gifts God has given us in this life, perhaps the greatest is the gift of parenthood. In an important way, it is as parents that we were made in His image. Though God creates by the word of His mouth, parents share in His creative power, bringing children into the world through their physical union.

There's no greater joy, yet at the same time no greater potential for sorrow, than being a parent. There are times in which my suffering has been great. But through the experience of parenthood I've come to know so well Him who is our heavenly parent and in whom we live and move and have our being (Acts 17:28).

In a sermon I occasionally ask the grandparents in the congregation to raise their hands. Of course, usually a large number do so. Then I ask those who are parents to raise their hands. (The grandparents should keep their hands up at this point.) Finally I ask those in the congregation who are children to raise their hands. Initially only the young identify themselves—until I point out that although we're not all grandparents or parents, we are all children.

Some have told me that the greatest loss which can be suffered in this life is the death of a child. I haven't had the experience, but I believe I can appreciate what this might mean. Someone has said that being a parent means forever walking around with your heart on the outside. There is no greater love.

If someone asked you where in the Bible the love chapter is, you'd rightly answer 1 Corinthians 13. Like the miracle of life itself, love is a mystery. This is because God is love, and His essence is beyond our comprehension. Although love cannot be defined, the Bible describes how it operates. The devil has for all practical purposes taken over the word "love," and unless we go to the Bible to test it, we'll be badly deceived. But we can always identify the real thing. It is long-suffering, kind, not jealous or proud, unselfish, has no hidden agenda, doesn't lose its temper, doesn't rejoice in the suffering of others, and loves truth. This description hardly describes what is being passed off as love in contemporary society. Being a parent is helping me recognize and develop true love.

Although I respect those who have chosen not to have children and have compassion for those who have not been able to, I thank God He saw fit to make me a parent. God had an only begotten Son. Because His Son was victorious through Him, so may I be too—as my Father's son. And if they choose, so also may be my sons and daughters. No matter the mistakes of the past, in Christ we—God's sons and daughters—may be more than conquerors (Rom. 8:37).

When you began to read this book you may have thought that by the time you got to the last chapter all your questions would be answered, all your problems would be over, and you'd soon see your children become ministers and Bible workers. I wish it were that easy.

We're on a journey that will not end until Jesus makes all things new. After the apostle Paul states the importance of love and describes what it is like, he ends by saying that when everything else is gone, there will be three things that remain—faith, hope, and love—but the greatest of the three is love.

When I contemplate these three great gifts of the Holy Spirit, I realize that although love is the greatest, it's nurtured by faith and hope. Without faith and hope, love does not grow; yet without love, faith and hope are worthless.

It is my love for my children that drives me to pray, "Lord, keep Your mansions; just save my children." Yet it is my faith in God and my hope in a new beginning that keep me praying. "But thus saith the Lord, Even the captives of the mighty shall be taken away, and the prey of the terrible shall be delivered: for I will contend with him that contendeth with thee, and I will save thy children" (Isa. 49:25).

On the surface this promise seems to be saying that all our children will be saved. Some are under the impression that Ellen White assures us that the last thing Jesus will do in His mediatorial work will be to save the children who have wandered away from the Lord. I'm sad to say that, according to the White Estate, this quotation does not exist. (See http://www.whiteestate.org/issues.) Nevertheless, of this one thing we can be sure—as long as the heavenly door of mercy is ajar the Holy Spirit will be working to save our children.

Some stories in Scripture make it appear as though God were trying to destroy certain people, and heroes of faith had to plead for their salvation. A case in point is our Lord's conversation with Abraham just before the destruction of Sodom. It seemed that Abraham was the only one who cared. But God knew the true condition of Sodom and agreed to spare it if there were even 10 righteous persons living there. The beautiful part of the story is that it soon became apparent that God was not willing that any should perish but that all should come to repentance (2 Peter 3:9). God had no intention of destroying the righteous with the wicked. He knew that a few persons would come out, but He also knew that to leave the civilizations of the plain intact would result in spreading the plague of sin that these cities had institutionalized.

When we reach the land of beginning again, I don't know which of my family members will be there. I'm not the judge of these things. But along with Abraham, I know that the Judge of all the earth will do right (Gen. 18:25). I will know, no matter the outcome, that the Holy Spirit will have made the supreme effort to save our family, and throughout eternity this knowledge will give me peace.

As we come to the close of this book I must tell you what happened after I took my son to the emergency room. He was put into a treatment program as an inpatient for two weeks. Afterward supervised outpatient care continued for several months, and mandatory meetings and testing will continue for five years. But the bottom line is that my son, who was dead in trespasses and sins, is alive again. The Lord healed our son, and for that we will praise Him forever!

Yet I have other children and grandchildren in spiritual danger, and the battle for our family continues to rage. Winning one battle doesn't mean we won't have to fight many more. The Scriptures caution us: "Be sober, be vigilant; because your adversary the devil, as a roaring lion, walketh about, seeking whom he may devour" (1 Peter 5:8).

When I attended Al-Anon I learned a prayer that is profound in its meaning and implications:

> *"God, grant me the serenity to accept the things*
> *I cannot change,*
> *the courage to change the things I can,*
> *And the wisdom to know the difference."*—Reinhold
> Niebuhr.

As we pray that God will save our children, the principles contained in the Serenity Prayer put things in the perspective that this book has meant to convey. As God works in the lives of our children, so He must work in our own lives, and we must permit Him to do both.

Earlier I mentioned the words of the old spiritual "Nobody Knows the Trouble I've Seen." If our eyes could be opened, we'd realize that everyone knows the trouble I've seen, because in one way or another we're all going through troubles. But by God's grace we must determine that "neither death, nor life, nor angels, nor principalities, nor powers, nor things present, nor things to come, nor height, nor depth, nor any other creature, shall be able to separate us from the love of God, which is in Christ Jesus our Lord" (Rom. 8:38, 39).

I close with these words: "For the which cause I also suffer these things: nevertheless I am not ashamed: for I know whom I have believed, and am persuaded that he is able to keep that which I have committed [our lives and our children's] unto him against that day" (2 Tim. 1:12).

CONSIDER THESE THINGS

1. We will not know the true meaning of love until we put love for God first.
2. One of the greatest privileges God has given is parenthood. In it He shares His creative power.
3. As with life, the essence of love is a mystery. We can only describe how it manifests itself.
4. While the Holy Spirit still strives with humanity there is hope for our children.
5. We don't need to worry. God loves our children even more than we do.

DISCUSS WITH SOMEONE

1. In what ways has the world distorted the true meaning of love?
2. How can praying the Serenity Prayer make practical changes in your life?

A PARENT'S PRAYER

Lord, we are so thankful for the wonderful gift of Your love. Because of Your love for us we have faith and hope. We pray that the Holy Spirit will keep Your love in our hearts—not what the world calls love but the kind of love You have revealed to us in 1 Corinthians 13.

We recognize that Your love does not for the time being solve all our problems, but it gives us the grace and strength to be able to continue. As You give us life from day to day, give us the peace to accept the things that we ourselves cannot change. In the meantime give us the will and the courage to allow You to change the things in our lives that need to be changed.

You have promised that if anyone lacks wisdom You will give it—liberally. We ask for wisdom right now. Lord, we have said You can keep Your mansions. You know what we mean. We're only saying we recognize that the most important things in this life are not prestige or wealth but the children You have given us. Lord, we recognize that only You can save us and our children, and for this we will trust You. In Jesus' name, amen and amen.

Destination Leadership

For Boards

Destination Leadership For Boards

Bill Geist

Neverland Publishing
Madison, Wisconsin

DESTINATION LEADERSHIP
for Boards

Bill Geist

Published by:
Neverland Publishing
PO Box 45445
Madison, Wisconsin 53744

Printed in the United States of America

Cover design and layout: Ad Graphics, Inc., Tulsa, OK

ISBN-10: 0-9755484-0-9
ISBN-13: 978-0-9755484-0-0

For My Girls

Contents

Before We Get Started:

THE DESTINATION MARKETING WORLD is awash in acronyms (see exhibit A at the close of this book) and a specialized lingo that often bewilders those that peer in from the outside. Unless you are an industry veteran, try to resist the temptation to jump ahead before reviewing the following definitions:

DMO. Our definitions start off with one that is currently evolving from one meaning to another (how's that for confusing?). DMO stands for "Destination Marketing Organization"... or, at least it used to.

In its original incarnation, a DMO was the organization that was the designated marketer of its destination. Through advertising, public relations, group and convention sales (and a myriad of other tactics and strategies), DMOs marketed their destinations to the rest of the world.

DMO is also an umbrella term that takes into consideration all the various titles that are used by organizations that are dedicated to marketing their destinations, such as:

- CVB: Convention & Visitors Bureau

- CVA: Convention & Visitors Association (or Authority)

- VCB: Visitors & Convention Bureau

- CTC: Convention & Tourism Corporation

- CTB: Convention & Tourism Bureau

- TB: Tourism Bureau

- TDA: Tourism Development Authority (or Association)

- TC: Tourism Council

In addition, there are Chambers of Commerce that, in the absence of a separate DMO, provide this service to their community. Sometimes Economic Development agencies provide DMO-like services. And, in an increasing number of communities, the traditional CVB moniker has been dropped in favor of a hipper, more stylish identifier such as NYC & Company, LA, Inc., Tourism Vancouver, Experience Columbus and Destination Bloomington. Some DMOs, capitalizing on the impact the web has had on Destination Marketing, have dropped the conventional CVB tag in favor of using their URL as the organization name, such as Wisconsin's VisitBeloit.com.

Bottom Line: There is no single phrase that works to identify the collective universe of organizations whose mission it is to attract visitors to town. Thus, the umbrella term "Destination Marketing Organization" (or DMO).

But even the DMO identifier is going through a subtle change in the minds of destination professionals around the world. For a growing number of organizations, the "M" now stands for "Management." And here's why:

Destination Marketing Organizations are charged with a maddeningly complex task that few, if any other, organizations must face. DMOs must market and sell a "product" over which they have no control. They cannot control size, quality or price. They cannot control availability, arbitrary governmental restrictions or complete product development. How many other organizations do you know that have their hands that tied?

Thus, many DMOs are electing to flex their collective muscle and assume a greater role in their communities. After all, no one else is advocating for the kinds of development that would enhance the destination's competitive position in the marketplace. No one else is inserting themselves into discussions at City Hall to insure that the redevelopment of Main Street takes into consideration curb cuts for taxis and motorcoaches.

If the destination is to flourish, somebody must take charge to insure that it happens. And, increasingly, that "somebody" is the Destination *Management* Organization,

It's still a DMO...but with a bigger, more important role in its community.

In this book, we'll use "DMO" to refer to the organization that markets its community to the rest of the world. If your DMO has made the jump to Destination *Management*, congratulations. You're still a DMO, but you're having a bigger impact on your community.

Destination Development: Taking the DMO conundrum (are we marketing or are we management?) to its logical conclusion, many DMOs are faced with the concept of "Destination Development." This concept can also be viewed in different ways.

For the Grant County/Marion (IN) CVB, destination development in the late 1990s meant developing an exceptional level of customer service throughout the County. The Bureau identified that its most cost-effective development strategy would not be trying to build a Convention Center but, rather, get visitors to Marion talking to their friends back home about how wonderful the people were in this destination, famous for its James Dean heritage.

Despite Marion's impressive advancements with this strategy, we will use the phrase "Destination Development" in this book to mean development of a more "physical" type. Convention Centers, Sports Stadiums, Marina Development, Waterfront Redevelopment, Downtown Revitalization, Visitor Centers, Airport Expansion...these are the bricks and mortar types of developments that can propel a destination forward.

There are, to be sure, smaller, more subtle development projects that can have significant impacts on a destination. Façade Renovation programs, Directional (or Wayfaring) Signage and Nighttime Lighting projects are just a few of the possibilities.

For the purposes of this book, when we say "Destination Development," these are the kinds of projects to which we refer.

Room Tax: It's called a lot of different things. Hotel Tax. Transient Occupancy Tax (or TOT). Bed Tax. It's all the same thing. A tax on the right of furnishing rooms for rent to visitors, paid by hotels, motels, resorts, B&Bs and any other facility that isn't somehow exempted. The City of Manitowoc (WI) even considered levying the tax on a restored WWII submarine in their harbor that offers onboard berths for the night!

Whatever it's called in your town, it's one of the largest funding mechanisms currently utilized by DMOs around the world. How it's invested is also one of the largest bones of contention in most destinations.

Whatever you call it, we're gonna call it Room Tax in this book.

Enough with the definitions. Let's get into the meat of Destination Leadership!

Introduction

IN THE DAYS AFTER SEPTEMBER 11TH, those Americans who were paying attention to the economy got a glimpse of what keeps this country prosperous. As the airlines were grounded, business travel restricted, meetings and conventions cancelled and as consumers quit purchasing experience, it became painfully clear how important Travel and Tourism is to an economy.

Before the attack, only a thin minority of business, community and political leaders appreciated the Travel Industry for the massive economic generator it is. Most looked upon travel as something they did for fun...and how, they reasoned, could something fun drive an economy? Others held tight to the belief that manufacturing was still king. Still others focused all their attention on high-tech opportunities they believed would be the path to the promised land.

When travel **STOPPED** in the United States, virtually every other industry ground to a halt, too.

But we are a forgetful society. At this writing, things are pretty much back to normal for most Americans...and we're traveling in numbers not seen since 2000.

And that brief moment when community leaders saw the impact that (the lack of) Travel and Tourism had on their destination? It, too, has faded from memory for all but a very special few in each town.

You are a member of that very special few. You have an understanding that there is something magical about an industry that works on so many different levels:

- Tourism infuses new money into a community's economy

- Tourism introduces prospective residents and businesses to a community or region

- Tourism is the face that we show the rest of the world (which is crucial for countries with a less than positive world image)

- Tourism Developments provide attractions and facilities for residents to enjoy

- Tourism generated taxes help keep resident-paid property taxes lower

- and most Urban Tourism attractions and venues make our downtowns attractive to the young professionals that every community should be trying to attract

No other industry touches as many facets of a community as Travel and Tourism. And, thus, no other community organization impacts as many people as a DMO.

So why is it that most DMOs don't have the respect of the communities they serve? Why are DMOs often not included in the discussions held by community leadership on defining the proverbial "next step?" Why are DMOs, as Greater Madison (WI) CVB CEO Deb Archer pointed out in a recent interview, "near the bottom of the food chain?"

Part of the problem is that Tourism is a "horizontal industry," cutting across countless sub-industries (such as dining, lodging, transportation, entertainment, nightspots, museums, etc.). Thus, identifying and quantifying these diverse sub-industries is difficult for those who are not familiar with the fact that they all feed into a larger hospitality industry.

Indeed, one could make a case that tourism is the ultimate horizontal industry...one that touches *every* other industry in the community. Go ahead. Pick a business in your town. They benefit from visitors.

Insurance Companies? They insure tourism-based businesses AND the cars, homes and lives of many in the hospitality industry.

Dry Cleaners? Wait staff uniforms and tablecloths.

Construction Companies? Well, who builds the attractions, the roads and the hotels?

Auto Dealers? Look in the employee parking areas of your largest attractions and shopping areas. An awful lot of the cars you see are sold and serviced at *local* dealerships.

Funeral Home? In my early days in the travel and tourism industry, I saw that a friend from college who managed his family's funeral home was a member of his local CVB...and *was listed in their Visitors Guide*. As I tried to stifle a laugh, I called my long lost fraternity brother to give him a hard time about trolling for clients via the visitors guide.

"I'm surprised at you," he said. "Don't you understand that tourism raises the wealth and prosperity of the entire community? My membership helps that happen."

He was, of course, as my friends in Northwest Ontario say, "bang on." More visitors to the community meant more community wealth...which, in turn, meant he could sell nicer caskets.

Now, I don't think that more expensive caskets was his primary reason for joining his CVB. He is a much bigger picture thinker than that. But the resulting wealth of a tourism-rich community surely wouldn't hurt his business...now would it?

Like I said...Tourism Touches Everyone.

Another issue that prevents many from seeing the importance of the industry is that 99% of tourism businesses are "small businesses," as classified by the Small Business Administration. Individually, our businesses aren't as well known as the local foundry, department store or bank.

This is troublesome on the one hand because small business owners are, well, small business owners. They are rarely the power elite in a community. And, thus, they are rarely consulted on their views because they are considered to be small potatoes.

On the other hand, small business owners work harder than almost anybody else. When do they have the time or the energy to call on political or community leaders?

Thus, whether it is that the power elite doesn't recognize the small business owner or the small business owner is too swamped to capture the attention of the power brokers, the tourism business is often overlooked. This is the reason why Tourism is often called "the Invisible Industry."

Over the past hundred years, the power elite in our communities have generally gravitated toward serving on the Chamber of Commerce Board. It's where you find the CEOs of banks, manufacturing and big business. Sometimes these power elite may drift over to the Board of the Economic Development Council in town.

The CVB / DMO Board has often been viewed as the weakling cousin to the more powerful Chamber of Commerce. The Chamber is always at "the table" when the important discussions are taking place...but the DMO is often an after thought.

When it comes to dollar-and-cents Return-on-Investment (ROI), this situation couldn't be more backwards. With no disrespect to Chambers of Commerce (for they serve a valuable purpose in today's destinations), there is no organization more crucial to the economic health of a community than its DMO.

No other entity has as immediate of an impact (promotional dollars in, visitor spending out). No other entity is more devoted to, or effective in, creating a compelling image for its hometown (after all, tourism is the face we display to the rest of the world). And no other entity has the impact on property taxes that a DMO has.

The Chamber may be where the power elite *think* they should be sitting. But, if they really want to have an impact on their community, they'll find their way to the DMO Board... like you have.

If you serve on a DMO Board, you are the keeper of the flame. You are responsible for advancing a vision for the future. Your community deserves no less.

You may feel that you are not prepared. You may believe that you don't have "the juice" to make things happen. If so, you are wrong, my friend.

For you *do* have what it takes. You answered the call to serve on the most important community Board on which you will ever serve. Period. You will look back on these days as the ones in which you had a significant influence on your town. And you will look back with pride.

There's no turning back or shirking this role. For, if not you... who? If not today...when? Your community (without knowing it) is depending on you...now more than ever.

For we, as the Boards of Destination Marketing Organizations, are the one, true force for exciting and positive growth in our communities.

You've been handed a rare opportunity. Let's begin...

Bill Geist
Madison, WI

CHAPTER 1

The Non-Profit Board

THERE ARE COUNTLESS BOOKS that cover the subject of the non-profit Board...and it seems that new ones emerge every month.

This is not one of those books. "Destination Leadership" focuses solely on the Destination Marketing Organization... and its unique form of governance.

Having said that, there are some basic maxims that are common to both entities...and we'll review them quickly in this Chapter so that there is a common understanding from which to grow and enhance the DMO Board.

A Non-Profit Board is the elected or appointed body that "owns and directs" the association on behalf of its constituency. Like a for-profit corporation, the Board is the ultimate authority, answerable to the stockholders (or, in our case, the "stakeholders").

Most importantly, a nonprofit Board establishes, monitors and (when appropriate) updates the vision and mission* of the association. It engages in regular introspection to insure that the association is meeting the needs of its constituents. It also

---

* Two very distinct concepts in the success of an organization. Vision is what propels an association forward (i.e., our dreams for tomorrow) while Mission keeps the organization focused on the job at hand.

looks to the future through strategic planning and visioning to insure that it is ready to meet the challenges ahead.

The nonprofit Board cannot effectively do all this alone. So, it identifies and hires a professional Chief Executive Officer (CEO), President or Executive Director. Once the CEO is in place, the Board must clearly identify its expectations to its paid professional and then monitor the effectiveness of, and provide support and resources to, its CEO.

On behalf of its stakeholders, the non-profit board oversees the financial condition of the association, approving the annual budget, major purchases and acquisitions. It sets policies that include legal and ethical directives for itself and its professional staff.

The Board also maintains the public standing of and the good-will toward the association. While the media and many key community influencers often view the CEO as the public face and voice of the organization, it is ultimately the Board's responsibility to insure that the long-range image of the association is a positive one.

Often left until last in most lists of its responsibilities is the very real requirement that the nonprofit Board must insure its own future success through succession planning, nomination and selection of new Board members and the effective orientation of these "new recruits." Indeed, nonprofit governance expert John Carver (author of the seminal book on the subject, *Boards that Make a Difference*) maintains that this may well be the most important function of a Board of Directors.

After all, if a long distance runner does not eat and drink to maintain his strength, he can't very well be expected to run a marathon next week. Carver holds that the same is true for Boards. You might be successful today, but if you fail to keep a steady stream of competent leaders in the pipeline, the association will fail in the years ahead.

Among the issues with which every nonprofit association must come to grip, we believe the following are crucial to the organization's long-range chances for success:

- **The Candidate Nomination Process must be formalized and held in the highest regard by the Board.** The Board must set criteria for nomination, establish a formal process (see Chapter 5) and never take the serious nature of this process for granted.

- **Every Board Member should have (and understand) their written job description.** Serving on a nonprofit Board is not an honorary reward. Even though you are not being paid, you've got a job to do. A formal description of the job and the organization's expectations of you are critical to the success of the association.

- **Spend Board time on the future...not the past.** Beyond providing a boring experience around the Board table, listening to a litany of reports does absolutely nothing to advance an organization. Outside of taking pride in a successful initiative or being able to lump criticism on a program that did not live up to expectations, a Board can't actually DO anything about the report. It's in the past! Instead, Boards should focus their valuable time together discussing how they will impact the future.

- **Keep your eye on the future.** Only by removing itself from the reactive day-to-day oversight of the organization can a nonprofit Board succeed in making a lasting difference in its community. The best

Boards are passionate about long-range Strategic Planning and will update their goals and strategies every 2-3 years, at a minimum.

- **Clearly identify the boundary between Board Governance and Professional Management.** In other words, the Board must avoid the pitfall of micro-managing its CEO. At the same time, it must avoid abdicating its role to a strong paid executive. A Board that gets involved in picking the color for the ads or insists on sitting in on every hiring decision is just as damaging to an organization as a Board that allows the CEO to make *all* the key decisions. The line between lax and micro is a fine one (and often shifting from year to year, based on the key issues facing the association)...and the Board and CEO must be clear on where that line is for the organization to succeed.

- **Make sure the staff compensation plan is competitive.** Good CEOs are becoming harder and harder to find. Smart Boards will not only consider what other exceptional nonprofit executives are making in the local market but also attempt to keep pace with industry norms. In today's ultra-mobile marketplace, organizations can face losing a stellar executive to another part of the country in which compensation levels may be higher than those in your region.

- **The Board "owns" the organization.** While it is true that Board members of nonprofit associations are not compensated for their services (as are many of their for-profit counterparts), the nonprofit Board member is far more than a volunteer. Being a "Volunteer" connotes a certain *laissez faire* level of assistance and a diminished degree of importance. Nothing could be further from the truth. The Board is the ultimate power in the organizational structure. If it believes that it is there to merely "help," the Board forfeits the ability to effectively wield this power to generate a lasting benefit to its constituents.

- **The Board is responsible for its own success.** A Board is delusional if it believes that the success of the organization is centered on its CEO. But most Boards allow the CEO to set the agenda for meetings and expect their executive to monitor and drive Board growth. Listen carefully. The Board is, as John Carver so eloquently stated in *Boards That Make a Difference*, "responsible for its own development, its own job design, its own discipline and its own performance." Board members who do not accept this role should step away from their seats and let somebody else contribute their unique time and talents to the organization. And, for those that refuse to step away, it's the Board's responsibility to remove them for the sake of the organization. Or, as Disney says (as they let their non-performers go), "invite them to find their future elsewhere."

- **Board Committees exist to do Board work...not to help with Staff responsibilities.** While tempting, Board members must refrain from participating in committees that focus on programming decisions. Board involvement in these committees often confuses the line between advice and direction for members of the professional staff. Boards should only participate in Board Committees such as Budget, Nominating and Strategic Planning.

These are just a few of the key issues facing today's non-profit organizations...and the Boards that lead them. If the science of Board Governance intrigues you, I recommend the works of John Carver and Doug Eadie (*Boards That Work*) to provide a deeper understanding of this topic.

As we mentioned at the top of this Chapter, DMO Boards are a unique subset of the entire nonprofit world. Thus, the general tenets of nonprofit governance apply.

But, the DMO world carries with it an additional set of responsibilities and challenges. And we'll address these in the chapters ahead.

CHAPTER 2

The DMO

WHILE THE BASIC CONCEPTS of non-profit organization Boards hold true for Destination Marketing Organization Boards, one must understand that DMOs are a strange mutant niche in the non-profit world due, in large part, to the way they are funded.

Case in point: there are precious few non-profit organizations that maintain contracts with governmental entities. Even fewer are the recipients of six, seven or eight figure sums of tax revenue with which they are expected to execute their program of work.

And, therein lies the rub. For the vast majority of DMOs in which government invests funds, that investment is viewed by most observers as "tax revenue."

Never mind that this tax revenue (for the most part) is generated from an industry that has been singled out for taxation by politicians who see this tax as one that will have limited (if any) impact on their re-election campaigns...because the people who pay these "hospitality" taxes don't vote (at least not in their district). And, never mind that this is a tax that residents generally don't pay. It is still viewed by Joe & Jill Public as "tax revenue."

Joe & Jill probably don't understand the nuances of how these taxes are different from the ones they pay. They also never give a second thought to who is inviting visitors to town... nor that visitors are crucial to the local economy. They don't consider that, if not for a DMO's efforts, customers wouldn't appear at our doorstep. Local businesses wouldn't be as profitable. New businesses would be slower to launch and grow. All that means fewer entertainment options for residents. And fewer jobs.

The end goal of a tourism strategy is increased visitor spending of new dollars in a community.

It also means fewer new dollars circulating through the community. Fewer dollars mean fewer taxes generated. And fewer tax dollars means either higher taxes for Joe and Jill or a reduced level of government services. In the end, without visitors, their quality of life suffers.

Here's how it works:

The end goal of a tourism strategy is increased visitor spending of new dollars in a community. The taxes on those new dollars being spent throughout the community on meals, entertainment, gifts and lodging benefit local and state government...and create a situation in which they now have new revenues to provide much needed municipal, county and state services. And maybe, just maybe, homeowner property taxes won't have to increase as rapidly as they would without visitor spending powering the economy.

Indeed, many states have calculated the tax impact to homeowners if there were no tourism dollars flowing into the community. And, depending on the size of the state, those impacts range from $400 to $1000 per year on the average home. Those are dollars that would need to come from taxpayers just to maintain the level of services they enjoy today. So, again, tourism touches everybody.

But Joe and Jill (and, unfortunately, many business and political leaders) still look at all this as *general* tax revenue.

And that complicates what should be an easy set of objectives for DMOs:

- Build the Organization
- Build the Destination
- Attract Visitors

But, before we begin, we must note that up to a quarter of all DMOs may not strictly follow the non-profit Board model. According to the most recent research from Destination Marketing Association International (DMAI), as many as 5% of its members operate as a division of a Chamber of Commerce. Another 19% operate as a division of municipal, county, state or provincial government.

As such, it is likely that these DMOs are loosely governed by an "Advisory Board"...and ultimately governed by another entity. In the case of government oversight, that ultimate authority may be the Mayor, County Executive or a governmental council or board. In the case of a parent Economic Development agency, the ultimate authority is likely vested in the parent agency's Board.

For the Board members of these minority varieties of DMOs, some of the norms, maxims and recommendations outlined in the following pages may not be as dead on as they will be for your independent 501(c)(6) non-profit Board brethren. But hang with us. You'll still pick up valuable insights into what makes a DMO Board click. (And spend some time with the Chapter 2.1 and 2.2 sidebars for our recommendations on the future of your DMO).

SIDEBAR / CHAPTER 2.1

SUBSIDIARY DMOS

The subsidiary DMO is a dying breed. While the first pure and independent Convention & Visitors Bureau was established in Detroit back in 1896, it wasn't until the 1970s and '80s that the CVB phenomenon took hold in North America. Prior to this time, the function of tourism promotion and development generally fell to the Chamber of Commerce. After all, this was the organization charged with community "boosterism" and, in the less competitive era before man walked on the moon (now *that's* tourism), such efforts primarily centered on passing out brochures and maps to visitors who stumbled into the Chamber office.

But, as the Interstate system connected America like never before and air travel became a commodity available to virtually everyone, we rapidly evolved into the travel-hungry society we are today.

As we hit the highways and skyways, an ever increasing number of lodging properties sprang up to welcome road and air weary travelers at the end of their days. Business travelers began to crisscross the nation in record numbers. Within a few years, the concept of levying a room tax on these lodging properties spread across the land. And, for the communities with a politically engaged hospitality industry, a portion, if not all, of the room taxes generated from this new tax were dedicated to attracting even more visitors to the community.

And then came the inevitable split. The Chambers, that had

maintained a modest little Tourism Committee to oversee the distribution of brochures and maps, now often saw these committees armed with bigger budgets than the mothership. And, with a bigger budget (thought many of the members of these Tourism Committees, who had bristled for years at their second class status within the organization), who needs the Chamber?

And, as the first Tourism Committees split from their parent Chambers, it became increasingly obvious to competitive communities that these new DMOs were becoming more effective in their sales and marketing efforts. It was not simply because they were independent but, rather, because they could apply laser-beam focus to their efforts in the highly specialized destination marketing side of economic development rather than working the entire economic development field.

As the remaining Chamber-represented destinations watched these more focused DMO-represented destinations lure their business base away, they began to petition their Cities, Counties and Chambers to spin the Destination Marketing function off to an independent sales and marketing focused organization. And, with the availability of Room Tax revenue to power these new organizations, most communities did just that by 1990.

To be sure, there are still some successful Chamber/DMO combinations out there, such as Asheville (NC), Door County (WI) and Myrtle Beach (SC). But they are successful because of clearly delineated lines of focus, control and budgeting. When Destination Sales and Marketing is just one of a number of Chamber initiatives (and not

Continued on next page

a clearly defined division), the chances are slim that they will be as successful as they could be as an independent entity.

Every few years, there appears to be a resurgence in Chamber attempts to "merge" with their local DMO. The rationale is sound to the lay person: "We can save on administrative overlap, payroll duplication and web design if we just all come together under one roof." Often times, the Chamber will suggest that the Economic Development Council (which also outgrew the Chamber's oversight during the 70s and 80s and struck out on *its* own) be part of this "bold, new umbrella organization."

Sounds good in its broad brush description...but it often is simply an attempt by a Chamber to get its hands on much needed new revenues. You see, Chambers

have great brand recognition. You go into business, you join the Chamber. It's what all good business people are supposed to do, right? It's kind of like Arm & Hammer Baking Soda. You have a 'fridge? You need to put an open box of Arm & Hammer in the fridge. Why? Nobody knows... you're just supposed to. Same thing with Chambers. You just do.

But today's young business leaders aren't buying the "cause-you're supposed-to" rap. They wanna know "why." And, in the case of many Chambers across the land, there is no longer a compelling answer. Most Chambers can't claim that they promote the community to visitors and conventions because the DMO does that. Many can't claim that they sell new companies on the notion of locating their business in the community because the Economic Development Council does that. So what can they claim?

That they're the voice of business? OK...but who's listening? Without an aggressive political advocacy program (which many Chambers unfortunately lack), it's a hollow concept.

That they encourage member-to-member business and referrals? Sorry, but in the new e-conomy, most of us are doing business with our global peers...and not the member down the street (unless she is the best choice on the planet).

That there are (like my Chamber points out on its website) "intangible benefits?" I'm sure there are...but, again, in today's world, I need more proof to be a member.

While some visionary Chambers have realized that their role has changed significantly over the past decade (and are aggressively pursuing new initiatives on behalf of their communities), the rest have lost their *raison d'etre*. And, until they understand that their purpose in this new millennium is vastly different than what it was after the Korean War, they will continue to drift aimlessly through their communities, taking on water as they continue to hemorrhage members that no longer see enough of a benefit to write one more dues check.

And, as these non-visionary Chambers continue to struggle, merging with them is a recipe for destination disaster.

SIDEBAR / CHAPTER 2.2

GOVERNMENTAL DMOs

For governmental DMOs, the organization's genesis often occurred as the municipality or county levied its room tax for the first time. In most cases, the Chambers in these destinations had done the brochure and map-passing thing for years, just as their counterparts across North America had done. Government had rarely dabbled in this field.

But now, with a pot of room tax money before them, politicians in these destinations had two thoughts. Unfortunately, for communities that currently have their DMO ensconced within the halls of government, one of these was not to encourage the creation of an independent DMO.

Instead, the thought process went like this:

1) "These are tax revenues. We must retain oversight. It is our civic duty. The voters would demand no less. The way to do that is to create a City or County Department." Sometimes this happened because the Mayor or Council had a control problem. Other times it was a turf issue (usually when the City and Chamber didn't get along).

2) Or, government saw this new Room Tax as a way to plug budget holes or fund pet projects without raising taxes (which would have resulted, if the electorate was paying attention, in them getting unelected).

Either way, it was a bad idea.

Don't get me wrong. Government does a magnificent job at what it does best: Services. From refuse collection to water sanitation to street and sidewalk maintenance to police and fire protection, most local governments rock. It's what they do!

There is a significant cultural difference between private and public and it stems from the fact that the private sector can't levy taxes. When it needs money, it has to earn it (which entails marketing and sales).

The public sector has never learned how to market and sell...because they don't have to! When the public sector needs money, it simply passes a tax increase.

Government no more understands sales and marketing than they know how to cure cancer. It's not in their genetic make-up. Say ROI to most public sector employees and they'll think you mean that outfitter store near the mall or the guy down in the mailroom named Roy. So, having a successful public sector DMO is like asking fish to fly. I'm not saying it can't be done...but flying fish are rather rare.

And, because government is usually big on control, the DMO Board is rarely anything more than an "advisory" council, often with only a token nod to including key industry representatives. Without possessing a strong business background AND without any real authority to make something happen, participation by the private sector is kept to a minimum. And, thus, many governmental DMOs forfeit the collective brainpower and clout that their independent counterparts enjoy.

When government is serious about generating an economic impact in its destination, it knows that it is ill equipped to take the lead. It contracts with an outside agency that has the connections, experience and ability to do the job right and effectively...with a high ROI.

But what about accountability? What about insuring that the tax funds provided for tourism promotion and development

Continued on next page

are expended properly by the private sector DMO?

The answer is disarmingly simple. It's called a contract. The government outlines what it wants in a document, the DMO agrees to perform as requested and the two parties sign it. Written properly, a legally binding document such as this would certainly go farther to insure the proper expenditure of tax revenues than letting the Mayor or the City Council administer the program.

I know I've painted a pretty dim view of governmental DMOs. Like the analogy I used, some fish *can* fly. It's just rare.

If your DMO is running smoothly and effectively as a governmental agency, congratulations. But it won't last. A change in the political power structure, a shift in public opinion or a severe budget deficit climate can change your "good thang" in a New York minute.

Consider moving the operation into an independent 501(c)(6) structure. It provides more opportunities to leverage resources, protects the mission from the ravages of politics and is more nimble when market conditions require a quick change in tactics and strategy. Nowhere was this more evident than in the first few years of the new millennium. The combination of a faltering economy and the terrorist attacks of 9/11 forced most DMOs to rapidly change gears and refocus their marketing and sales efforts. Entities that were ensconced in a bureaucratic cocoon struggled to make the changes that were necessary in those rapidly changing times.

And don't worry about loss of control. A carefully worded contractual agreement between government and independent DMO will provide more control than most in-house operations ever could.

THE ORGANIZATION

Non-profit Boards exist to provide guidance and oversight over an enterprise that is not designed to turn a profit. Put another way, a Non-Profit Board acts as the Stockholders or the owners of the company.

In the case of philanthropic or social service non-profits, Boards help fundraising for worthy causes and then advise professional staff on the proper and most effective ways to invest the monies. In the case of Trade Associations, the Board (made up of association members or industry partners) develops and oversees a program of work that would make them more profitable.

DMOs are a variation of the Trade Association model. It is true that some of its primary beneficiaries are businesses within the destination that benefit from visitor spending. And, to this end, a lot of what a DMO Board does is spent listening to these destination partners in an effort to direct the organization's efforts to create more business for these stakeholders.

But it goes so much further than that (or, at least it should). A DMO Board is also, by its very nature, responsible to the entire community. And, here's how it works (for most destinations):

A community levies a Room Tax (or other hospitality related tax) to generate the necessary funds with which it can invest in a competitive strategy to attract visitors to town. Leisure Travelers. Convention Attendees. Motorcoaches. Sports Events. Film Crews. You name it. If they don't live here...we want them to visit. A veteran Convention Center Director in the Northwest hit the nail squarely on the head when he said, "We invite people to town. We pick their pockets. And we send 'em home with a smile."

Now, because the hotels are "collecting" the room tax, they believe that the lion's share of the revenue invested in a DMO should be focused on putting "heads in beds." And, to a certain degree, they have a point. Not because it's "their money" that's being used (it's not), but because the overnight guest tends to spend more money in the community than the "daytripper" (and, thus, delivers a higher ROI).

But, the governmental entity that enacts the tax doesn't do it to make sure the hotels are full. They do it to bring visitor dollars to town...and the taxes they'll generate while here*. That's the bottom line for any politician (besides getting re-elected): balance the budget. And visitor generated dollars come in mighty handy when you're trying to show the locals that you're "holding the line" on tax increases while providing more governmental services.

There are only a handful of industries that are taxed in addition to the obligatory sales tax, hotels being the most popular target. And, if hotel tax revenues aren't reinvested in efforts to increase visitation, then it is clear that the taxing authority is taking advantage of an industry's customers that don't live within the region. For, if the customers of the hotel object to this additional tax, they have no recourse (as proffered by the founding fathers). They cannot vote the bum(s) out of office because the vast majority of those staying in hotels can't vote in local elections.

Of course, what the politicians in these clueless communities don't realize is that these customers CAN vote...and they do it, not by the ballot box but, in a more impactful manner. They refuse to return for future visits, choosing to spend their dollars elsewhere. And meeting planners, event planners, motorcoach

---

* Of course, some governments enact these taxes solely to generate cash...with no consideration of the potential ROI of investing it in Destination Marketing. These governmental entities are being sensationally short-sighted...and exhibit a disturbing lack of civic ethics.

operators, corporations and savvy leisure visitors do just that when they perceive the room tax rate to be too high for the benefits they receive from the destination and its DMO. And, they tell their friends. And then, they tell the world on TripAdvisor.com, their blogs and their online social networks.

The "Heads in Beds" axiom is repeated from DMO Boardroom to Boardroom across the land. But, it's also "Cheeks in Seats," "Torsos through Turnstiles" and more "Cha-Ching" at the registers that are the pre-requisites of a vibrant tourism economy. After all, only 13% of the average visitor dollar is spent in hotels. Up to 32% is spent in retail establishments and roughly 26% is spent in restaurants. To focus only on hotels would be ludicrous, but to ignore them is to under-achieve.

Indeed, for many destinations, a sizable percent of the visitors never step foot in a hotel. They are VFR (Visiting Friends and Relatives). But, just because they aren't sleeping in a hotel tonight, are they any less important of a visitor to our economy?

> *...it's also "Cheeks in Seats," "Torsos through Turnstiles" and more "Cha-Ching" at the registers that are the pre-requisites of a vibrant tourism economy.*

What happens when friends and relatives stay at your place? Don't you take them out to dinner, a show, an attraction or two? And don't you all go shopping at least one day? VFR tourists, while not over-nighting in a hotel, are an important piece of the visitor impact pie.

Which is why a DMO Board must be about more than just filling hotel rooms. It's gotta be about bringing the most people to town for the most reasons over the most days...which varies greatly from destination to destination.

So...how does the DMO Board achieve this?

For most, it's about selecting the most qualified CEO and arming that individual with the most resources possible. And those resources can range from financial assets to destination infrastructure.

Let's start with financial resources. It's up to the Board to make a compelling case for the investment of governmental dollars into the DMO's program of work. Assuming there is a Room Tax or Hotel Assessment in place (and, virtually 90% of destinations have one), that revenue must be reinvested in tourism promotion and development so the community realizes the greatest return on this asset.

Some communities impose food and beverage taxes. Others levy rental car taxes. In California, Tourism-specific Business Improvement Districts (BIDs) have been created to power DMO marketing in many cities. Whatever taxes and fees are collected from visitors, a DMO Board must make a compelling case for these funds being reinvested back into the marketing and development of the industry.

But, beyond public funding of a DMO, there is the opportunity to use public dollars to leverage private investment... and that traditionally comes in the form of partnership agreements.

Often referred to as "Membership," co-operative partnerships offer a number of provocative benefits to a DMO. Obviously, it increases the size of the DMO's operational budget.

Beyond money, however, a partnership program offers a number of other benefits to a Destination Marketing Organization. Opponents of the practice of investing in DMOs will have significantly less solid ground on which to stand if faced with the fact that the DMO is successful in generating "match money." Indeed, the majority of those who oppose the investment of room tax dollars into DMO programs tend to be those who perennially have *their* hand out for government subsidization. Few can claim a significant private sector investment match and, so, their arguments lose some luster.

Providing the opportunity for private sector investment also opens doors for non-traditional partners to become involved with their DMO. During my tenure as a CVB CEO, a local car dealership was the biggest single corporate investor in the Bureau...bigger than our biggest hotels, bigger than our largest attractions. They were our partners because we brought events to town through which they saw promotional opportunity. And while they were big supporters of the local Chamber of Commerce...they invested more dollars in their CVB.

Another advantage of private sector partner investment is the participatory involvement that it brings to the organization. It's one thing if a DMO represents a business. It's quite another if that business has invested money into the organization. The *laissez faire* attitude of the former is replaced by the latter's invigorated involvement in the DMO.

Businesses that are invested partners are more likely to appear at City Council and County Board meetings than their non-invested peers. They're more likely to participate in the development of leisure packages and convention or event bids. And, they are more likely to expect the moon.

While we certainly support the concept of private sector partnership, we must caution that some "members" expect an awful lot for their $250. To be sure, these partners tend to be the "mom and pop" variety businesses that count pennies rather than Franklins. And, paraphrasing the Pareto Principle*, these members can produce a majority of your DMO's headaches, despite having only a modest impact on your budget.

The "80:20 rule" has become one of the best known "leadership shorthand terms" reflecting the notion that most

* *Pareto's Principle: Vilfredo Pareto was an Italian economist who studied the distribution of wealth and discovered a common phenomenon: about 80% of the wealth in most countries was controlled by a consistent minority — about 20% of the people. His observation eventually became known as either the "80:20 rule" or "Pareto's Principle."*

of the results come from a minority of effort. Reversing this equation, many have argued that 80% of your problems come from 20% of your income/clients. And so it often is in DMO membership programs.

In fact, it is this overriding level of member expectation that sets many DMOs apart from other non-profit associations. But, the advantages of an aggressive partnership program to a DMO in terms of public and political support, marketing connectivity and cooperation and competitive intelligence sharing can make it worth the hassle.

Besides the Pareto Principle, there is one other caution. Membership dues are often the lifeblood of the Chamber of Commerce. In communities with a limited business base, a DMO membership program can be viewed as a threat to the Chamber's funding base. The potential for a nasty little turf battle could be deadly for some DMOs.

Which is why you may have noted that I have often used the word "partnership" in the preceding paragraphs, rather then "membership," to describe the marketing and revenue opportunities before DMOs. Over the past few years, there has been a growing trend among DMOs to evolve their traditional membership programs into partnership programs.

The philosophy behind this move is that "Membership" connotes being a part of a club that provides a set of "benefits." On the other hand, "Partnership" connotes a joining together of two entities with common goals and the understanding that, together, they are better able to hit those targets. As a DMO, which would you rather cultivate?

Partnership programs also allow the DMO to establish "investment levels" instead of "dues." It paves the way for developing customized levels of marketing visibility for varying levels of investment. It opens up the chance to design sponsorship and co-op programs. And, it reinforces the true nature of the best possible relationship between DMO and business. Not as an entity in service to its members but, rather, as an organization working *with* area businesses to expand the reach and frequency of its sales and marketing initiatives.

THE DESTINATION

Beyond the financial assets and professional marketing management required to effectively promote a destination, a DMO Board should also search for ways to enhance the infrastructure of the destination.

As we've said before, Joe & Jill Public don't always get it. Neither do many elected officials and, thus, governmental employees. And precious few community leaders understand. It is up to the DMO Board to be the advocates for smart and unique destination development in our communities.

Here's an example that is, unfortunately, all too typical in our communities. The Chamber of Commerce (or the City or the Downtown Merchants Association, etc.) unveils its "2020" plan for the community. It features renovated

> *...a DMO Board should also search for ways to enhance the infrastructure of the destination.*

office buildings. It has some pretty landscaping. It has a new parking deck. It has a new Performing Arts Center. It has lots of "stuff."

What it doesn't have is a strategy to turn this "stuff" into a compelling visitor magnet because that's just not the way they think. Their plans don't reserve first floor spaces in office buildings for restaurants, nightspots and retail. Their plans don't include the proper electrical hook-ups in the landscaping for compelling night lighting or "plug and play" access for entertainers. Their plan doesn't take into consideration the proper traffic flow, signage or curb cuts for cabs and buses around the Performing Arts Center and their parking is four blocks away (but close to the big office building)...because they're thinking *locally*, and not *destinationaly*.

To paraphrase the Hebrew scholar Hillel, "if not us, who? If not now, when?" And those questions need to be asked by every DMO Board in the land. If you don't champion developments that will increase interest in your community, who will? And, with the rising level of competition out there, do you really have the luxury of time to wait to see if somebody else might advance a plan with visitors in mind?

Outside of building a kick-butt organization, a DMO Board's most important function is that of advocate and champion of Destination Development.

And, in its most basic, boiled down form...that's what a DMO Board does. It doesn't choose the ads or help create the marketing plan. It doesn't design the promotional brochures or the website. You've got staff that can do that. Duplicating efforts does nothing but slow your progress. Do something that no one else can do...**BUILD** the **ORGANIZATION & THE DESTINATION!**

And we'll show you how in the pages to come....

CHAPTER 3

Who Does What

NOW COMES THE TOUGH PART. We know what we are and what the effective DMO Organization is expected to do. So, who's responsible for seeing that it's done?

As one of my professors in Business School once said, you can answer virtually any question in macro-economics with, "that depends." This isn't meant to be a dodge to an extremely thorny question. But there are no "cookie-cutter" solutions to this dilemma. Indeed, "who does what" will change in every destination, depending on the key issues before the destination and the cast of characters that have been assembled.

But, take heart, there are some constants...and we'll touch upon those before we delve into the more subtle nuances of Destination Leadership:

VISION & MISSION

As we've already noted, a DMO Board owns and directs the enterprise on behalf of the destination. Just as for-profit corporations, the DMO Board must set and regularly reaffirm or shift its Vision and Mission.

Coca-Cola's Vision was once "a Coke within arm's reach of every person on the planet." That pretty much says it all.

Your Vision Statement should be just as bold (without being clearly unattainable*).

While *Vision* is what you want to be, *Mission* is what you will do to get there.

Put another way, a DMO Board meets and takes action because they have a *Vision* for the future. And, every decision they make should be in alignment with their *Mission* Statement in order to keep them on track to reach that Vision.

> **While Vision is what you want to be, Mission is what you will do to get there.**

Your DMO's Mission Statement is a crucial tool to keep the organization laser-focused. Without a clear Mission Statement, the organization can, in good faith, try each and every cool idea it develops in order to "see what happens." To avoid the old adage, "if you don't know where you're going, any road will take you there," the successful DMO needs to know where it is going in order to make the smartest decisions.

In the year after winning the public referendum to build the Frank Lloyd Wright-designed Convention Center, the Greater Madison CVB began to suffer from "Mission Creep." Consumed with the Convention Center effort for the previous two years, the Board had yet to focus its attention on the "now what?" question. Thus, it was easy for them to support a proposal to launch a world-class Marathon. Indeed, they hadn't begun to think about what the next iteration of the organization should be (i.e., a DMO focused on selling the city as a meetings and conventions destination).

---

* I once participated in a Strategic Planning session in which the facilitator refused to allow any semblance of reality temper the Vision Statement process. We ended up with the following Vision: "Wisconsin will be the pre-eminent destination in the galaxy." Remember, there's a difference between being visionary...and absurd.

In the weeks after the Marathon, most observers would have categorized the event as a major success. Running publications gushed over the first-year numbers and quality of the event. News and feature coverage of the event was exceptional. But, those of us close to the event winced at the realization that we had just expended a significant amount of staff, volunteer and sponsorship resources on an event that generated an estimate $275,000 of visitor impact for the community.

Forget the seed money. Forget the sponsor dollars and volunteer hours that could have been better utilized elsewhere. We dedicated one and a half full-time staff positions for a full year...for a return to the community of $275,000 in visitor spending? That's about the impact of a two-day convention of 100 delegates.

Had we not been so hazy on our true Mission in the days after winning the referendum vote, the 1.5 persons we dedicated to the Marathon would have been out selling meetings and conventions...and, conservatively, would have generated *$10 million* in visitor spending. The silver lining of the Madison Marathon? It cured our case of "Mission Creep" real fast.

GOAL SETTING

In addition to establishing Vision and Mission for the organization, there are two types of Goals with which a DMO Board should concern itself: Strategic (long-range) and Tactical (short-range).

Strategic Goal-setting often requires the Board to schedule an "all hands on deck" Annual Retreat to stretch out and honestly discuss, debate and decide the future of the organization and the destination. But the Goals that are set in these retreats are *Board Goals*. These traditionally involve enhancements to the destination's infrastructure, increasing the organization's budget and other initiatives that are big picture, destination-altering in scope.

On the other hand, Tactical Goals are those that drive staff to a higher level of performance. These may be Room Night Goals for the Sales Department, Repeat Business Goals for the Convention Services Division, Inquiry and Internet Goals for the Marketing Director or Media Placement Goals for the Public Relations staffer.

The Board should not set Tactical Goals...the CEO should. And here's why. Outside of the select Board members that represent tourism businesses and may have some insight into market factors, the Board doesn't have anything more to base its decisions on than the previous year's performance numbers. And, putting a wet finger to the air and coming up with an arbitrary 10% increase goal over prior year productivity is just a wishful guess.

The CEO should, in concert with her staff, develop a set of Goals for the approaching year. They have a greater sense of the markets in which they work on a daily basis. They have access to competitive intelligence from other DMOs in the region and national trend services. They know if the Convention Center is already 75% booked for the upcoming year and, thus, that they'd be in a position to produce a higher ROI for the destination if they sold less meetings business and more sports tournaments. In short, the CEO and staff are in the best position to suggest goals that are aggressive, yet realistic.

To be sure, the Board must review these goals with the CEO and, if appropriate, approve them. If the Board believes the Tactical Goals to be too soft, it should communicate its concern to the CEO. In turn, the CEO should reconvene the staff and discuss whether they believe they can do better. If the CEO and staff honestly believe that they are already pushing the envelope as far as it can go, the Board needs to take this assessment seriously. In most cases, however, the CEO and staff, with the encouragement of the Board, will rise to the challenge.

COMMUNICATING CLEAR EXPECTATIONS

And this leads us to the critical need for clear, concise communication between the Board and its CEO. An effective Board of Destination Leaders will advise the CEO, in no uncertain terms, the level of productivity it expects *and the measures it will utilize to assess performance.*

When a CEO clearly understands the Board's expectations, he'll apply a much sharper focus to his own goal setting. If he is told that the Board expects more conventions than the year prior, he'll develop a plan to meet that expectation. However, if he knows that he'll be measured against room night productivity, he'll design and/or approve marketing and sales initiatives that specifically focus on high value customers that can produce the largest overnight events.

In return, the CEO must communicate clearly with the Board. If he thinks that the Board's belief that the medical meetings niche holds unlimited promise is based upon faulty data, he needs to explain why he disagrees. The Board, in turn, must take his concerns seriously and work to find common ground. After all, the Board hired a professional destination marketer, presumably based upon its belief that he was the best qualified individual for the job. Unless he has exhibited a pattern of shirking goals and suggestions from the Board, he deserves the benefit of the doubt.

NOW...WHO DOES WHAT?

Outside of establishing Vision and Mission Statements, setting Strategic Goals and approving Tactical Goals, one of the biggest issues before a DMO Board is the division of duties (who does what). For some reason, it seems like DMO Boards struggle with micro-management issues more than your garden-variety non-profit association Boards. Maybe it's because our work seems fun. Marketing. Promotions. Events. Development. It's sexy stuff compared to many social service non-profits.

Maybe it's because many of the people on DMO Boards are attraction marketers in their own right. Some want to share their success secrets. Others may want to direct DMO resources in such a way that it benefits them more directly than their competitors.

Whatever the reason, it bears discussion because it seems to happen so often. And, the smart Destination Leaders will take a firm stance on the separation of Board and Staff.

No one says it any clearer than governance guru John Carver: "The Board has only one employee. The CEO has the rest."

In other words, as much as you'd like to, the Board should not be interacting with staff. Period.

Every time a Board member and a staffer communicate, it weakens the separation of "church and state" that has been created for a number of very good reasons. Among the unwanted consequences of Board-Staff contact:

- **Staff confusion.** A Board Member encourages a staffer to change the primary color of the ad to blue. The CEO hates blue and has already told staff to use only the approved Destination "color palette" on all ads and communiqués. But, the staffer fears that the Board Member has more authority and could get him canned. But, if he uses blue, the CEO will pop her cork.

- **Lack of Accountability.** The Board Marketing Committee instructs the Marketing Director to advertise in Portuguese travel publications...against his better judgment. After six months, not a single inquiry can be traced back to the ads. The Committee complains to the CEO that her Marketing Director should be fired, despite the fact that he objected to the concept in the first place.

- **Internal Conflict.** After a year or so of regular communications at Board Meetings, the marginally-motivated Director of Convention Sales believes he has a friend in one of the Board Members. When he misses his quarterly goals and fails to receive his bonus, he complains to the Board Member that the CEO's compensation program is a joke. Pretty soon, the Board member begins sharing the staffer's gossip and "insider-information" with other Board Members...one of whom has an axe to grind with the CEO. Within weeks, the chain of command begins to disintegrate.

Think about it from your business' point of view. Do your managers appreciate you bypassing them and offering operational suggestions to their direct reports (especially if they are different from their standing instructions)? Do you want disgruntled staffers going around their supervisors and taking their complaints to you?

Face it, the process is most effective when the Board has one direct report...the CEO. It also saves you the time-consumptive hassle of sorting out who did or didn't do what they were supposed to do. If the DMO is hitting its marks, you've likely hired an effective CEO.

If the DMO chronically falls short of its goals (and there are no apparent industry or economic anomalies at work) and the CEO fails to make the necessary adjustments in staffing or strategy, it's time to search for a new CEO. It's that simple. Boards that realize they are responsible for just one employee don't get mired in the minutia...and can use their time more productively on behalf of the Destination.

Thus, you need a strong and accomplished executive to handle the myriad of issues before the organization. If your CEO can take care of the business, the Board can focus on the future.

Which brings us back to the "Who Does What" Question. In its simplest form, the answer goes like this:

• The CEO and Staff do the Marketing, Sales and Service.

• The DMO Board of Directors focuses its attention on the types of things that have the potential to change the Destination. These traditionally fall into two distinct areas: Organizational & Destinational. An Organizational agenda focuses on building the DMO's budget and influence. A Destinational agenda focuses on advocating for infrastructure and service developments designed to make the community more attractive to visitors.

THE ROLE OF COMMITTEES

We, like Carver and Eadie, are not big fans of Board Committees. Outside of Board Development and Budget & Finance, we're not sure why good Boards need committees. After all, if the Board is engaged and pro-active, every member should be current on the major issues before the organization. While a study-group or task force may make sense to investigate a new opportunity on behalf of the Board, these short-term groups do not qualify as "standing committees."

However, we are BIG proponents of *organizational* committees that lie *outside* of the Board. These are committees that advise and assist staff. The CEO may report on the various committees' work to the Board from time to time...but these committees are not under the direct purview of the Board.

A prime example of the difference between a Board Committee and an Organization Committee would be the seemingly ever-present "Marketing Committee." Should this be a Board Committee or an Organization Committee?

If you said "Board," that's the "wrong answer" buzzer that you're hearing. While Marketing is what a DMO does, making Marketing decisions is the role of the paid professional executive and her staff...and NOT the role of the Board. After all, if the Board makes the marketing decisions, why does it need a CEO? And, if a Board makes the marketing decisions, how can it assess the results of its CEO? One can imagine a Board Marketing Committee directing a CEO to place 40% of her advertising budget in the local paper (because the publisher sits on the Board) and then chastising her (or worse) when visitor inquiries (and, thus, conversions) plummet.

Does this mean DMOs shouldn't have Marketing Committees? No. Just not at the Board level. A Marketing Committee that advises the CEO and her staff is, as the Wizard said, "a horse of a different color." As long as the Committee is devoid of Board members (so that there can be no misunderstanding of whether an idea is a "suggestion" or a "direction"), we're big proponents of Marketing Committees, Convention Sales Committees, Membership Committees, etc.

Member or Partner-based Committees can provide sensational ideas, competitive intelligence and industry support for DMOs. Let's continue with the Marketing Committee as our example. With a Committee made up of your brightest marketing executives from area attractions, hotels and other businesses, the DMO benefits from thousands of dollars of "consulting time" from these professionals. One may have discovered a great way to increase e-mail newsletter "open rates" in her company that she's willing to share with the DMO. Another may have seen a great destination promotion on his last cross-country trip. These are ideas, tactics and solutions that the DMO marketing staff may never have thought of...but could be adapted successfully for future destination promotions.

These Committee members can also provide meaningful insight into the periods in which they could really use the business...or alert the DMO to hold off on a promotion because the hotels are already virtually sold out for a particular period. The intelligence that the members of such a Committee could provide is invaluable.

And, finally, when Committee suggestions and ideas are incorporated into a DMO's program of work, the organization gains a powerful cheering section back in the hospitality industry. For, when professionals see their ideas acted upon, they become supporters of the organization, even when others question its activities. Active Committees can create fabulous buy-in from industry partners throughout the destination.

Just keep Board Members out of them. Boards have their role and work...and Committees have theirs.

I know this concept is a hard one for Board members to get their arms around. Especially when it comes to marketing, because that's the fun stuff!

And this should give Board members pause. Where do *you* want to contribute? If your expertise is sales, maybe you should serve on the Convention Sales Committee and not the Board. You may be in a position, because of your knowledge of industry trends, sales tactics and the Association Market, to make a significantly bigger impact on the DMO (and, thus, your community) by serving on that Committee than on the Board.

While this book is about Boards and Destination Leadership, serving on a Board is not all its cracked up to be. If you can check your ego at the door, you may find that your role is somewhere else within the organization.

Bottom line: If your strengths lie in the tactical (short-term) realm...consider volunteering for a committee. If your strengths lie in the strategic (long-term) arena where building the destination and the organization are primary considerations...the Board is where you belong.

CHAPTER 4

Designing
Board Structure

FIRST UP, WE MUST TACKLE the thorny issue of whether the Board is appointed, elected...or a mixture of the two. As we touched on in Chapter Two, governmental DMOs will generally appoint an "advisory board" (so called because the ultimate authority rarely resides with the Board but, rather, with the Chief Elected Official). The Mayor wants to make a change at the top? The Mayor can make the change.

But assuming that your DMO is not a governmental unit, the Board must do everything in its power to avoid the pitfall of appointed members controlling the majority of the seats and, thus, the conversation.

Governments, industry associations (such as the local inn-keepers, restaurateurs and attractions) and other special interest groups will lobby for seats on the Board. In many instances, DMO Boards have agreed that such representation would be (in theory) a good thing...and then have punted away the future by allowing too many of these groups to select *their* representatives for the newly created seats.

A DMO Board should never allow more than 50% of its seats to be chosen or appointed by those outside the Board.

This gets to a fundamental philosophy of Board governance: A Board made up of appointees cannot represent the best interests of the organization. They represent the interests of the appointers.

Think about it. The Mayor appoints 6. The County appoints 6. The Chamber appoints 3. And there are 3 at-large seats. And let's say the City is contemplating a significant reduction in its investment in the DMO.

> *A Board made up of appointees cannot represent the best interests of the organization. They represent the interests of the appointers.*

When push comes to shove, the Mayor will call in her chits from her 6 appointments. Assuming the County is also in a budget crunch and wants to maintain harmony with the City, those votes will block an objection from the DMO Board to the Mayor's proposed cuts. And, the Chamber, also wanting to stay on the Mayor's good side, will vote her way as well.

Now, let's look at a scenario where the City and County each have an appointment...as does the Chamber and the local Hotel Association. The other 14 seats are Board selected. The Mayor announces plans to cut the DMO budget.

The decision on whether to oppose the budget reduction will be made on the merits of the proposal. How will it affect the long term viability of the DMO and the destination? Does the Board believe it has a leg to stand on to fight back?

In other words, the Board will make the decision that is best for the organization at that point in time. Chances are, the Board may well agree to the reduction rather than go head to head with a strong Mayor. Or maybe they won't. But, either way, it is the *organization* talking...not someone that controls seats from the outside.

But (I hear you cry), what about the City's argument that it must have seats to oversee the tax revenues being invested in the DMO? Easy. Tell 'em they'll get all the oversight they need with a well written contract for services between the City and the DMO. In fact, the level of control will be greater with a contract because the Mayor won't have to worry about her appointees wiggling on her on a close, emotionally charged vote.

Of course, the Board can reinforce its trustworthiness by engaging a reputable outside firm to do annual financial audits (whether it's called for in the contract or not). In addition, performing organizational and performance reviews from time to time not only signals to your stakeholders that the DMO is serious about the very real business of tourism development but helps the organization improve its own effectiveness.

Indeed, an accreditation program has been initiated by Destination Marketing Association International. Called DMAP (Destination Marketing Accreditation Program), this rigorous process provides a method to assure staff, volunteer leadership and external stakeholders that the organization is following proper practices and performing at an acceptable level for the industry. And, while a DMAP certificate on your DMO's wall won't prevent every ethical misstep from happening, it surely proves to customers and stakeholders that your organization has systems and controls in place to prevent such an occurrence.

Despite the logic of this argument, there will be situations where the majority of the Board will continue to be appointed. Indeed, in some states, it's the prevailing law. In these cases, the Board must take a proactive role in appointment process. You cannot assume that the person responsible for appointing the Board knows what kind of individuals are most needed at a particular moment in time.

In these instances, Board leadership must go through the same process that we are about to outline for an effective Nominating process (short of the selection phase) and make its case for the best and brightest individuals you can find. The Mayor may not agree with all of your recommendations but, if you've developed a strong relationship, chances are she'll appreciate your suggestions and confirm many of them.

INDUSTRY AFFILIATION

When you strip the DMO Board and Mission down to its most basic role, it's about the creation of economic wealth and impact. All social, governmental and quality of life advantages flow from the creation of wealth. Thus, the first consideration should be the creation of a Board that represents the business community.

Note that I didn't say "tourism industry" or "hospitality industry." That's far too limiting if the Board is going to make an impression and leave a mark on the destination.

Many DMO Boards today are top-heavy with hospitality industry representation, most often in the form of hoteliers. And, on the surface, one could certainly attempt to make the point that they deserve to be a dominant force on the Board because, after all, it's "their money."

WRONG. Room Tax is *not* their money. Room Tax is a pass-through tax that hotels simply *collect* on behalf of the Municipality or County. And, despite popular opinion, hotels are *not* the primary benefactors of a vibrant tourism economy.

Of course, one could also look at this from a different point of view. If all the visitors stopped visiting tomorrow, what industry would go out of business first? Hotels, of course. On average, 95% of a hotel's revenue is derived from out-of-town visitors.

Now, before you start chuckling about the locally derived 5%, remember that at least some of that 5% is made up of food and beverage charges from local meetings, black-tie events, weddings and service club lunches. And...yes, a few people who are probably with somebody they shouldn't be.

And, of course, without hotels, visitors couldn't stay in our destinations as long as we'd like them to. And, it's a fact that the longer a visitor stays in a destination, the more money they leave behind for the community.

Unfortunately, it was that 95% dependency on visitor business that made hotels such a delectable target for lawmakers in the '70s and '80s. As previously mentioned, the majority of those taxed couldn't vote the taxers out of office. But, even more importantly, local residents, by and large, do not pay local hotel room tax. Taxes on food, beverage and entertainment are much harder to impose because they involve local spending. Sure, some visitors will pay the tax, but the lion's share falls on voters. And that is something that politicians in many communities are reticent to do.

So, while they do not reap the largest benefit from visitor spending, hotels depend far more on the visitor dollar than their peers in the rest of the hospitality industry. But should this earn them extra seats on a DMO Board?

No. While they clearly benefit from the work of a DMO, hotels do not automatically deserve the lion's share of the seats on a DMO Board because of this dependency for two basic reasons:

1) Hotels are not the only businesses that benefit from a vibrant tourism economy and,

2) Hoteliers, by the very nature of their business, tend to have a very short-term bias in their view of the world.

This is by no means a shot at hoteliers. Hotels are *vital* to our mission of drawing more visitors to the community in that they are where these visitors will sleep. And sleep they must if the destination is to reap the highest impact possible from the visitors.

Someone once said that hoteliers tend to focus on the next Quarter while DMO Boards should focus on the next Quarter Century. And, since a growing number of hotel executives in our communities represent out-of-market ownership, their very livelihood is, understandably, based upon short-term results.

When Madison began its final push to build the Frank Lloyd Wright designed Monona Terrace Convention Center, a number of hoteliers were vociferous opponents. They feared that the Center would pull meeting business away from them and attract a developer of new Headquarters Hotel. Never mind that the Center would be generating tens of thousands of new room nights for them (room nights they would never be able to attract without the Center). They just feared a potential loss in food and beverage business and the chance that a new competitor might elect to build a hotel downtown.

Because of these fears, the local Hotel/Motel Association was split on whether to support the referendum. To their credit, the majority saw the big picture. But, had hoteliers made up a majority of the CVB Board, the Convention Center would never have been built because the Bureau could have never taken the lead on the project.

Today, there is not a hotel in town that isn't benefiting from the Convention Center (even *with* a new Headquarters hotel next door). The downtown has ignited into the place to be and be seen. Where half of the storefronts surrounding the Capitol Square were boarded up in 1990, there isn't a square foot available to rent today. In the 15 years since the referendum win, over $500 million of *private sector money* has been invested in the downtown.

A DMO Board should be focused on long-term results. A DMO Board controlled by hoteliers will have a short-term bias. Even in this current economic climate in which the here and now tends to consume the discussions of many DMO Boards, the smart ones will be looking for future opportunities...not trying to plug the dike.

So...despite their intimate connection to a DMO's funding, hoteliers should make up no more than 25% of any DMO Board.

Why have any hoteliers on the Board, I hear you muse? They aren't generally "destination-focused," they're often out for themselves and many may try to force the organization into programs that are short-term fixes to their immediate needs.

Aye, but they bring a certain competitive intelligence to the table. They're in the front lines talking to the customer. They're behind the scenes, negotiating with the Convention Center. They are, in many cases, working with the same clients we are for meetings, conventions and sports events. They're often connected to lodging properties in other parts of the country and they are, after all, the business that will fail first if the tourism economy goes sour. They are the proverbial "Canary in the Coalmine."

And, government taxes them. If there is going to be a change in the rate of tax or, more importantly the distribution of the funds generated, the voice of the hotelier is crucial to the discussions of a DMO Board.

Hoteliers belong on the Board...but not in numbers as to be able to command a majority voice. That's asking for trouble.

So...What's the Best Structure:

Like my B-school professor said, "that depends." Every destination is different. But, we like to see a diverse Board of community leaders, thinkers, influencers and, yes, contrarians.

Here's what I think would be a perfect Board:

2 Hoteliers – One Full Service. One Limited Service. *Any more than two and you risk them trying to com-*

mand the conversation (because they get one more from an appointment from the Hotel Association).

1 Restaurateur – *The good ones tend to be adept at political advocacy and can be a wonderful asset...and they are often long-term residents*

1 Retailer – *We need them to learn the importance of tourism*

1 Attraction – *They are, after all, the reason people visit your destination*

1 Media Owner or GM – *a crucial support opportunity...with a powerful voice*

1 Arts/Cultural Leader – *whether they know it or not, they can be a significant attraction*

1 Financial Industry – *preferably a banker*

1 "Big Business" or Developer – *more than one and you'll risk being called a pawn by the progressive left*

1 Education – *College or Junior College preferred. High School is OK if they are in a position of curriculum leadership*

1 Association Executive – *they offer a unique view of the meetings and convention market*

1 Appointment from the City

1 Appointment from the County

1 Appointment from the Hotel Association

1 Appointment from the Restaurant Association

3 At-Large to satisfy geographic, gender, ethnic, age, handicapped and other critical diversity criteria that cannot be accomplished through the seat criteria

That's 18...and only 4 are appointed.

Still missing somebody crucial in your community? That's what ex-officio seats are designed to provide.

To recap, your job as a Destination Leader is to envision the future, advocate for appropriate destination enhancement and development and build a stronger organization.

One of the ways you can insure the latter is to focus some of your attention on building a better Board, which we'll cover in the next Chapter.

CHAPTER 5

Building the Board

MAX, THE CEO OF A MID-SIZED CVB, was blessed with a diverse and dedicated Board. But a comment made by one of his officers during a routine Board meeting rocked the organization.

The owner of the largest and most successful chain of restaurants in the region looked around the Board table at his peers and said, "we gotta get a better Board." As the rest of the Board glared at him, some in anger at his suggestion that they were somehow unworthy of their seats, he continued by saying, "and I'll be the first one to resign my seat to make way for a stronger set of leaders."

As I said, Max had a diverse and dedicated Board. But "dedicated" and "well-connected" aren't the same thing.

It's like the concept of "Six Degrees of Separation," in which a Harvard researcher suggested that the average number of personal contacts it takes to reach anyone else in the world is six. Selecting the proper six people, of course, is the trick. But, in theory at least, we are only six people away from knowing anyone on earth.

Most CVB Boards, if well designed, should operate in no more than a "Three Degrees of Separation" arena. In other words, each member should be able to touch a key opinion leader or decision maker in the destination in three phone calls or less. If the target is a large retail developer, Mark should be able to connect with that developer by calling Ann, who knows Bruce, who is tight with the target. Three Steps. Three Degrees.

> **If a Board member cannot influence those who have influence, one must ask what purpose that individual serves on the Board.**

The fewer the steps, the stronger the Board. If the majority of the Board is "Two Degrees," it's stronger than a "Three Degrees" Board. If a Board is "Four Degrees," it needs to recruit a more well-connected member base during the next Nominating Committee process. After all, if you are four or more phone calls away from the people that can get things done in town, what good are you to the organization?

I don't say this to offend...but to make you think. If a Board member cannot influence those who have influence, one must ask what purpose that individual serves on the Board.

We've seen Nominating Committees select PR professionals or marketing mavens because they know about advertising and promotion. That's wonderful...but if they can't influence governmental leaders and the power elite of the business community, they shouldn't be on the Board. They should be on a Committee. The Board exists to get things done. Committees exist to assist and advise staff. If you can't get things done, you shouldn't be on the Board.

As we've discussed, DMO Boards exist to enhance the destination, strengthen the organization and engage a professional CEO. Depending on which of these roles emerges as most important at a particular point in time, the organization should focus its attention on Board candidates that can most effectively advance that mission.

SIDE BAR

IF YOU'RE 4 DEGREES (OR MORE) AWAY...

Just because you're not three degrees or less away from "the juice" in your community, doesn't mean that you have to stay that way! If you believe that you're NOT in a position to influence the influencers in your town, take these steps to change the way you view yourself and the way others view you:

• **Get to know your local political leaders.** Find out who your City Council and/or County Board representative is...and find a way to meet them. While it sounds simplistic, you'd be surprised at how few residents have actually shaken the hand of their representatives... which means you'll stand out in their mind as someone that they've actually met.

Many of these positions are up for election every other year,

which means you'll have a perfect opportunity to catch them at a campaign appearance or coffee klatch at a local supporter's home. If you're between elections, look for their name in the media and call or e-mail them to voice your support on a position they've taken on which you agree. It doesn't have to be tourism related. In fact, it's better if it isn't, as they'll see you as a community supporter that has more than a single issue agenda.

Of course, calling to say that you think their recent vote on garbage pick-up was stupid won't produce the long range results that you desire. Wait until they support something you support so that you can find common ground. Then you can move on (in a few months) to the issues that are really important to you. Once

Continued on next page

you've laid the initial groundwork, they'll be more open to hearing your message.

• **Join a Service Club.** At the entryway to most communities, you'll find a sign bearing the logos of Rotary, Kiwanis, Optimists, Junior League, Jay-Cees, Sertoma and a myriad of other Service Club Chapters. Ask around. Which are the clubs in which the power elite of the community are members? Join one...
and then dive into the volunteer opportunities provided. You'll soon find that you are shoulder to shoulder with the people who are making a difference in your community.

And...so are you! And that provides a common bond that gives you the access to the movers and shakers in your community. And, if you don't end up shoulder to shoulder at the hot dog stand or the beer tent...chances are you will at the weekly meetings. Use these meetings to meet the influencers

in your community and, as with your politicians, begin this new relationship on a note of commonality. Bring your interest in the tourism industry's impact on the community to the table in the months ahead.

• **Get on another Board.** While the time you have to volunteer is limited, look for other non-tourism specific Boards on which you could serve. Again, search for the ones that include community leaders AND which you strongly support. Your presence on other Boards (or on the committees for these organizations) advances your ability to connect with "the juice" in the community.

Boards are not unlike professional sports teams...and a recent example comes to mind. The high-flying Green Bay Packers, sporting one of the best records in the NFL, sailed into the playoffs leading up to Super Bowl 37 (and when will they stop with the roman numerals thing?). They had never, in over 75 years, lost a post-season playoff game at home. They had one of the best quarterbacks in the history of the game. They were favored by more than a touchdown to win.

Instead, they got pounded in the first round by a team with a young, fast, run-and-gun quarterback.

> *...the best Boards are ones that bring a high level of influence and diversity to the table.*

During the off-season, the Packers focused their efforts on acquiring faster defensive players so that what happened to them on that cold January afternoon at Lambeau Field would never happen again.

Were there better players available in the college draft? Yup. Could they have traded for more accomplished veteran players? Sure. But, preparing for the coming season, they needed defensive players with speed. And that's where they focused their attention.

My point is that the smart DMO Board needs to understand what its primary role is before it begins to build the team that will take them there. Just because an individual is well liked, well placed or well connected doesn't mean that she is right for the Board at that particular moment in time.

That said, the best Boards are ones that bring a high level of influence and diversity to the table. As we've discussed, such "juice" is something that will need to be developed over time. But, one of the ways to develop this is through embracing the concept of diversity.

Industry. Gender. Race. Age. Geography. The list can be as long as you like. The Diversity you seek should be just as deep. In fact, there is a dizzying number of factors that need to be taken into consideration when building the effective DMO Board. And, chances are, you'll never be able to include individuals from every possible background on your Board.

But, that doesn't mean you shouldn't try. And here's how we suggest you start:

The Process of Building a Great Board:

It all starts with a sea change in the way we view the Nomination Committee process. In fact, Doug Eadie (in *Boards that Work*) suggests that the Nominating Committee be renamed the "Board Development Committee."

Whatever it's called, here's how it (unfortunately) usually works: Let's assume that Board terms begin on January 1st. Most Boards fire up their Nominating Committee in late August or September (and I'm being kind here, as we've seen some scrambling to get them up in October and November). Usually headed by the Immediate Past Chair and a handful of less than motivated Board members, the Committee starts calling friends and acquaintances looking for new blood that would be willing to join them on the Board.

"Oh, it's only one meeting a month," they plead or, "It's a fun group," they lie, trying to convince potential board members of how easy being a member of the Board is. But, as when a dentist says, "this won't hurt," the prospective board member only hears "this is gonna get ugly."

Is this any way to run one of the most important and vital organizations in the community? Of course not.

We propose a vastly different scenario:

For the purposes of our proposed timeline, we will use a January 1st start date. If your year differs, make the conversion in your head as we go.

FIRST QUARTER

As your Board welcomes its new members at the January meeting, the Board Chair should direct the Board Development Committee to begin its work. That's right...at the FIRST meeting of the year.

As we said earlier, what is more important than replenishing the organization's fuel? Identifying and landing new Board members is one of the most important things a Board does. So let's take it seriously.

During the first quarter, the Board Development Committee should identify the organization's upcoming needs. Ask questions like:

- Who is stepping off the Board?
- What industries or constituencies do they represent?
- What skills and connections do we need to replace or add to the mix?
- How can we increase the diversity of the Board?
- What areas do we need to augment, given the Board's stated goals over the next two years (remember the Green Bay Packers?)

Their deadline to complete this initial phase of the process: March 31st.

SECOND QUARTER

During the second quarter, the Committee moves from needs assessment to candidate identification. Each Committee member should arrive at the next meeting with a first and second choice candidate for each of the "needs" identified during the first quarter.

The goal for the Committee should be to develop a list of potential candidates that is at least double the number of available seats to be filled. In this way, the Committee will have flexibility should a candidate decline the invitation or emerge to be not as qualified as originally presumed.

The deadline for the Candidate Identification stage should be no later than June 30th.

THIRD QUARTER

Some Board veteran readers will say that they do these first two steps in the process already...and, to them, we say, "congratulations." You are members of an elite group of destination leaders who have taken a thoughtful look at your organization and are positioning your Board for future success.

But the next step is where many of even the best Boards falter: the Interview Stage. Instead of having a committee member who knows Maura call her to see if she might be persuaded to join the Board, a far more effective plan of attack is to have the committee member invite Maura to lunch. There, in a relaxed setting that should afford the two an hour or so of conversation time, the subject of the DMO and its role in the community can be discussed. Questions about the Board can be answered in a conversational environment. There's no pressure. This is a "look-see" opportunity for both individuals.

But, up front, this first meeting should lay out the bare minimums for Board Member involvement:

- Attendance at all Board Meetings
- Active participation in assigned Board Committees or Task Forces

- A willingness to advocate for the organization and the destination
- An adherence to a Board Ethics Policy*

If Maura agrees that she'd be interested in taking the process further *and* if the committee member still feels that Maura would be an appropriate and strategic addition to the Board, a formal interview should be scheduled. This time, the full Board Development Committee should meet Maura in a less casual setting, for this meeting is all business.

> *When this format is employed, an intriguing thing happens: the candidate begins to fight for the position.*

This gives both sides a chance to explain why they think the match is a good fit for the destination. It gives the Board a chance to stress the importance of the organization. It gives the candidates a chance to express the strengths that they can bring to the table. In short, it establishes that we are all professionals, coming together for the advancement of our community.

When this format is employed, an intriguing thing happens: the candidate begins to fight for the position.

It's another interesting facet of human nature, best exemplified by the classic Groucho Marx line, "I wouldn't want to join any club that would have me as a member." When someone

---

* *Destination Marketing Association International has developed a Standard of Conduct for DMOs. Whether your organization is a member or not (and we recommend that you are), you can adopt the Code as standard policy for your organization. Better yet, use it as a model and build your own Code to your more stringent specifications. Member or not, the Code is a service that DMAI has offered to the entire DMO industry as a way to encourage ethical behavior and standards for all in our profession. The DMAI Ethics Policy can be found in Chapter 10.*

is pursuing you, your interest is often nominal. When there's a chance that someone else may be selected instead of you, you dig in and start fighting. It's the competitive juices that flow through virtually every one of the successful individuals who are reading this book. We want to win...and if there's a chance that the DMO Board may select someone else, we'll become much more engaged in the process than we would if we were being pursued.

And isn't that exactly the kind of Board members we want to be sitting next to for the next three years? Engaged. Committed. Dedicated. By starting their relationship with the organization from a competitive platform, new Board members will be more energized than their peers who were merely pursued.

The Deadline for the Interview Phase: September 30. And start early...as summer is vacation time for most in the Northern Hemisphere.

And, as we discussed earlier, if your Board still falls into the "appointed" category, this is where the Board needs to approve a set of names to be recommended to the Mayor or County Executive for their consideration and action.

FOURTH QUARTER

While the process in the third quarter is the most time consuming, the fourth quarter simply flies by. The Committee has the intelligence of the candidate interviews. Those members of the candidate pool who, during the process, came to realize the time that would be involved in being a Board member was too much or that there just wasn't an appropriate fit between their interests and the DMO will have removed themselves from consideration.

Now, the Committee makes its decision...voting on the candidates who best match the Board needs that were identified in the first quarter. And, the candidates who emerge from that vote are forwarded to the full Board as the Board Development Committee's recommended slate of new directors.

The final slate represents the best, the brightest and the most capable individuals for the growth of the destination and the organization *at that point in time*. And the Board can be sure that it's getting the best because of the thoughtful process used by the Board Development Committee instead of the harried chase that characterizes most selection processes.

And, as it spreads the workload out over 10 months, members of the Board Development Committee won't get as stressed out (a good thing for Board morale).

Sure beats the way you've been doing it, doesn't it?

But, what to do with the ones who don't make the cut? They've come a long way with you over the past three or four months and this process has turned them into individuals who have actually sought the nomination. The last thing you want for those you thought highly enough of to initiate the interview process is for them to turn away from the organization hurt or angry. After all, DMOs have enough detractors in a community. You really don't want another who is smart, connected and capable.

Unless the individual wasn't selected because of a glaring flaw that was discovered in the interview process, look for ways to invite them to serve in another capacity in the organization such as a committee or a task force. The conversation might sound something like this:

"Lee, the Board met yesterday afternoon and, as you know, we had a number of extremely qualified and exciting candidates for a limited number of seats. With the Riverfront Redevelopment plan moving into the forefront of what we're going to be focusing on in the months ahead, the Board was compelled to elect Jackie to the seat we were looking at you to fill because of her close ties to the Mayor and several members of the Council.

"While I know the vote may be a disappointment, the Nominating Committee was very impressed with what you could bring to our organization, and we'd like to get you involved with our Public Affairs Committee to help keep the media focused on the importance of the Riverfront Project for all members of the community... not just tourists. And, while I can't promise anything, I'd certainly be surprised if the Board didn't turn to you for one of the open seats next year."

> First, for every candidate, the Board Development Committee should ask itself, "can we see this individual as Board Chair in four years?"

Of course, you should only offer that last line if you believe it to be true. Left at the altar once is bad enough...

SOME OTHER CONSIDERATIONS

Every incoming member of the Board should have the ability to become Board Chair...and I mean this in two distinctly different ways.

First, for *every* candidate, the Board Development Committee should ask itself, "can we see this individual as Board Chair in four years?" If the answer is no, why are you considering this person? If they aren't a strong enough candidate to one day lead the organization, we question your interest in them in the first place. Don't settle...shoot for the best of the best for your Board.

Secondly, on a more tactical basis, make sure that your Board terms and format don't preclude members from leadership positions. I was once involved with a Board that offered its members the chance to serve two two-year terms. The Chairmanship of the organization was a two-year term. Thus, assuming that most Boards would not elect a Board Member who was just finishing his first year on the Board to the Chairmanship of the organization, it was virtually impossible for anyone coming onto the Board in the middle of a Chair's term to ascend to a leadership position. Their first shot at the Chair would come too soon for them to be ready. The second shot would come too late, when they had only a year of eligibility left.

In addition, a two-year term format faces members who have barely gotten their feet wet with the decision of whether they want to re-up. And losing good people after only four years to a short term limit rule seems a waste.

Look at your By-Laws and term limit structure. Walk through the different scenarios to be sure that no one is being artificially blocked from leading the organization. Our favorite structure is two three-year terms.

Such a format provides for a first-year "learning-the-ropes" stage and two years of Board productivity. At the end of three years, some will feel they have contributed what they could and not seek another term. Most will be energized by their first three years and ask to stay on for three more. And, regardless of whether your organization prefers a one-year or two-year Chairmanship, the two three-year term format allows every member time to make a run at a leadership position, if they so desire.

Bottom Line: Are the terms long enough for board members to become skilled as destination and DMO leaders while being short enough to avoid "calcification" and the perception that the "power" in the organization is concentrated in an elite few? The two "3s" gets you there.

An exception to the rule: In some small-population destinations, the talent pool is somewhat limited. Depending upon the size of the destination and the Board, some DMOs might be better served with longer term limits. But, please, anything over ten years is asking for trouble.

THE EXPERTISE TRAP

Finally, as the Board Development Committee begins its work in identifying potential candidates, beware the "Expertise Trap." While it may be tempting to invite local "experts" into the mix, there are three downsides to having resident experts on a Board.

First, experts tend to dominate the conversation on their particular topic, causing others to withdraw from participating in the discussion for fear that their ideas on the subject may appear foolish. Second, experts are often driven by a narrow view of the world ("we've always done it like this" or "this is the only way it can work"). The most exciting projects are the ones that incorporate new and unique ideas. Unfortunately, those rarely come from experts.

Finally, experts often can't help themselves from micromanaging projects. While it's often with the best of intentions (hey, they're the "expert" and they just want to help), their involvement beyond setting goals and lining up community support can often de-evolve into directing staff work, thus blurring the lines of accountability in the organization.

Experts are a fabulous resource for DMO Boards...but they are often more effective and less disruptive as consultants *to* the Board rather than consultants *within* the Board. If you need expertise on a particular topic or project...create an advisory committee to cherry-pick the best ideas from the experts in your midst.

CHAPTER 6

Energizing the Board

SO WHAT SEPARATES "asleep at the wheel" Boards with the ones that accomplish great things? Beyond the roster of the DMO Board, the determining factor is often found in the Board meetings themselves.

As governance expert John Carver says in *Boards that Make a Difference*, "Board members arrive at the table with dreams... yet, by and large, (they) do not spend their time exploring, debating and defining those dreams."

In *Boards That Work*, Doug Eadie goes even further in his indictment of today's nonprofit Board when he says that they are "frequently ineffectual, reacting

What is a Sundial in the Shade?
– Ben Franklin

rather than leading, rubber-stamping rather than directing (and) enervating rather than energizing their members, providing a boring rather than a challenging experience."

Ben Franklin may have (unknowingly) described many non-profit Boards best when he penned these words: "What is a Sundial in the Shade?"

While it sounds simplistic, the schedule and format of Board meetings play a huge role in determining whether a DMO will be a Destination Leader...or just another waste of people's time and talent.

Scheduling.

Show me a Board that meets quarterly and, nine times out of ten, I'll show you a group of people that are not Destination Leaders. Don't get me wrong. I'm not saying that the organization can't be successful. A well-oiled organization with an accomplished CEO can make this format work. But the Board as Destination *Leaders*? Extremely doubtful. And here's why...

The world in which we live is far too complex and moves too rapidly for anyone to have an impact if they show up for a meeting every three months. Think about it. Let's say a Board is championing a destination project and votes to publicly support a funding plan for a new sports complex. A week after the meeting, a cartel of city council members comes up with a plan to lessen the property tax burden on residents by shifting room tax revenue away from the DMO to the bonds for the complex. In week three, the newspaper endorses the new plan as "visionary" and within days, the Mayor has switched his allegiance and is calling for a vote to approve the project in week five.

They'll be putting out an RFP (Request for Proposals) for contractors before the quarterly Board ever meets again. And don't tell me that calling an emergency meeting to deal with this flare-up is the answer. Destination Leaders don't call emergency meetings because they are in control of their world. The scenario above wouldn't have happened with a Board that took their role more seriously than getting together four times a year.

Oh, and on a side note: The practice of quarterly meetings also stinks because, inevitably, everybody has to miss a meeting once in a while. With a quarterly format, if you miss a meeting...you don't participate for half of a year!

Destination Leaders can get by with bi-monthly meetings if nothing significant is currently cooking. But, for most Destination Leaders, monthly meetings (with a month off during prime vacation months or December) are crucial if they are to leave a mark on their community.

The Agenda.

There are precious few Boards that design the agenda of their meetings, preferring to let the CEO prepare the content for discussion. After all, they say, the CEO has a better grasp of what we need to discuss than we do!

While that may be true, a CEO-designed agenda will often drift into two camps: items that are really staff issues and items that are of immediate interest to the CEO.

John Carver calls an agenda heavy with staff issues the "Approval Syndrome." Boards that don't take charge of their meeting agenda are often faced with a set of reports to consider and approve. How boring! The heavy lifting has already been done. All that's left for the Board is to approve, edit or reject somebody else's work. What a waste!

And, if the Board is discussing the issues important to the CEO, it risks being brought down to a staff decision level again. For, despite the best intentions of DMO executives, the things most important to them are often the issues that they are facing on a daily basis. Unless the DMO is involved in a destination development project or a political action to increase investment levels in the organization, chances are that the CEO will be discussing new program initiatives.

Even *if* the CEO is focusing on destination and organizational development issues, they are most likely tactical (short-range) in nature. As the effective DMO Board should be talking about strategic (longer-range) issues, it is imperative that the Board designs the agenda to avoid a myopic view of its world and miss the opportunities before it.

In the end, the Board cannot expect staff to tell them what they need to be talking about. If the Board understands the organization's role in the community, is dedicated to its mission and focused on a strategy for the future, it should know full well what it needs to talk about at its next meeting. The CEO can certainly assist in the preparation of the agenda (and should)...but the Board Chair or Executive Committee should be the initial authority on this topic.

For those Boards that still want an easier way out of the task of setting agendas, we offer the following thought. Chances are that your DMO's Strategic Plan has a number of primary Goals. Take the number of Goals and divide it into the number of meetings you expect to have in the coming year (for example, 3 goals into 12 meetings = 4).

You've just established the lion's share of your agendas for the year. And here's how the agenda will go: The first 10-15 minutes of the meeting are spent in approval and acceptance of minutes and financial data. Create some time (10 minutes) for a brief discussion or update on anything that the Board needs to know to be a better informed steward of the organization. And then, the rest of the January meeting will focus on the progress being made to achieve Goal One. In February, the agenda is exactly the same, except the majority of the time spent together is devoted to Goal Two...and so on.

Given 3 Goals and a monthly meeting schedule, the Board will "go deep" into the progress being made on each goal every quarter. More Goals? Fewer meetings? You can still adapt this agenda model.

If you have 4 Goals and semi-monthly meetings, do two Goals each meeting. 5 Goals and Quarterly meetings? Well, that begs the Quarterly Meeting question again...

The Meeting.

The best and most productive discussions involve divergent points of view. The effective DMO Board will embrace, honor and value diversity of thought. Not in a politically correct, group hug, sing Kum-Bah-Ya kind of way (that would result in "paralysis by analysis"). But, rather, to insure that all voices are heard before making a Board decision.

It's a Board culture that needs to be developed and nurtured...and the Board Chair is the one who must passionately pursue this hallmark of great Boards. Board meetings should be a place where contrarian views are encouraged. For, without the dissenters, decisions are made in a vacuum.

When everyone is in full agreement on a plan and the excitement is in the air, flaws in the concept are often overlooked. It takes someone to challenge his peers and make them fight for their plan to insure that it is, indeed, the correct path to pursue. While contrarians may not win the day for their side, they often make the plans they oppose better. They help us realize that not everyone is of the same mind. They help us refine the sharp edges that could offend or engender community-wide opposition.

In the end, the Board makes good things happen. And, then, a curious thing happens. Meeting attendance increases because the Board knows that something powerful is going on here. They begin to rearrange their schedules around Board meetings (rather than asking for Board meetings to be rescheduled around *their* calendar). They don't want to miss a minute... or a vote. It's exciting, invigorating and vital. They are part of an organization that is going to "leave a mark."

Putting Board Members in a Position to Lead.

Part of the energy that can be generated by an engaged DMO Board can be found through public visibility. The more visible the members of the Board are in the community, the more they'll contribute.

This happens for two reasons. First, the more a Board Member is seen by others, the more her "stock" rises in the community. Community leaders that may have only heard of her now see her on a regular basis. So does the media. Pretty soon, without ever meeting her, people are dropping her name as somebody that should be considered for this committee or that project. While the illicit video made her a household name, we first knew of Paris Hilton because she did nothing more than show up at a string of high-profile parties where other well-known people (and paparazzi) were. And, as Woody Allen said, "80% of success is showing up."

Secondly, visibility is also important because most of us rise to the top of our game when we're in public. We carry ourselves more purposefully and our senses are sharper when we know we're being watched. And, when people begin to expect us to be fabulous, we tend not to procrastinate or get sloppy. Public visibility makes us better at what we do because expectations are enhanced.

So, how do we achieve this visibility for ourselves, our DMO and our Destination? Be like Woody Allen and show up. Chamber Dinners. Urban League Events. Downtown Development Breakfasts. Major Ribbon Cuttings. Mayoral News Conferences (when they are related to the Destination). Anytime the Governor makes a visit to the community. These are all open to the public. Go!

But that's not all. The DMO needs to create its own public events at which Board Members can be seen. Quarterly News Conferences to announce impact statistics or new initiatives. Business-After-Hours events at member or partner businesses.* Destination events for which the DMO has provided support.

Between your visibility at Public and DMO-Sponsored events, your level of involvement, enthusiasm and connectivity with other community leaders will soar. And so will the image, effectiveness and clout of the organization.

---

* Just not strip clubs. A number of years ago, a CVB came under a barrage of media fire when some of its employees were filmed entering a Bureau Member Strip Club for an after-work reception. While everybody kept their clothes on, it was enough to cost the well-respected CEO his job and cast a pall of suspicion over the organization. More on this in Chapter 10.

CHAPTER 7

Your Level of Involvement

THE BOARD IS IN PLACE. You're ready to roll. But you have one more decision before you. How engaged will you be?

This is not a rhetorical question. Just because you are a member of a DMO Board doesn't mean that you have joined a fraternity of like-minded groups across the globe. Some Boards will be passive. Some will be advocates. Some will deftly work behind the scenes. And some will be, as Apple Fellow Guy Kawasaki once called them, "raging thunder-lizard evangelists."

There are extremely successful Boards out there that view their role as advisors and stewards, investing the lion's share of the visioning and implementation of the organization's plan of work in their CEO and his staff. The Board is content to set the organizational standards and goals, be ceremonial public figures as required and leave the heavy lifting up to the paid professionals.

While there are exceptions to every rule, this style of governance is usually the mark of a "good-old-boys" Board. And, while many CEOs may secretly wish for such a scenario, it does have some pitfalls attached (like everything that looks too good to be true).

Regardless of how accomplished and persuasive your CEO may be, he will almost always be viewed with a degree of skepticism. After all, it's his job to convince the community that Project X is a good idea. It's his job to persuade the City Council to increase its investment of Room Tax in the organization. And, in many cases, critics may harbor some resentment because he earns more than they think he should and/or he wasn't born in town and might leave when a better offer comes his way.

Of course, none of this has anything to do with the merits of the argument. But most disagreements in the public arena don't.

An active, visible Board that takes a public stand on critical issues goes a long way towards eliminating many of the petty objections that can be lobbed at the paid CEO. Especially when the public sees the owner of a non-tourism business (who played football at Central High twenty years ago and is a past president of Rotary) get up and advocate for Project X. It's just hard to argue with the resonance that such a well-positioned individual can have in advancing a position.

The other downside to a Board that hands the keys over to its CEO is that, some day, somebody on the Board is gonna want a bigger role. The CEO will have become comfortable running the show and may not be interested in changing the modus operandi for this individual. The Board, comfortable in its "supporting" role, will also not race to change the status quo. And the new Board member will start to pick away at the edges, trying to get a foothold from which to change the way business is done in the organization.

Once again, it's a human nature thing. If a Board member feels blocked, she may decide to question the CEO's effectiveness. If she is adept at creating subterfuge, other Board members may chime in and, in no time, a small cancer has formed that could threaten to go public. Once public, the media will play the division within the Board for all it's worth... and the organization will become a target of community-wide skepticism.

All because somebody wanted a little more say in how the good-old-boy organization was run.

Beyond these two rather tactical reasons why passive Boards leave a lot to be desired, a much bigger picture should motivate today's Destination Leaders to take hold of the reigns of their organization. It's called creating the future...and nobody is in a better position to do it than the members of the DMO Board.

> *The opportunity to collectively discuss, debate and decide the future with some of the best, the brightest and the most dedicated community minds in the destination is powerful stuff.*

It's one of the reasons that we encourage the Boards we work with to dispense with all the reports of staff activity that traditionally consume Board Meetings. These reports chronicle what has already happened. Thus, the Board is squandering its attention listening to something that cannot be changed.

What a waste of valuable time! If the average salary of your Board is $150,000, that breaks out to $72/hour per person. If your Board numbers 18, that's roughly $1300 of high level brain power squandered during a meeting in which the Board listens to a series of reports. Over a 10-meeting year, that's $13,000 of consulting value wasted...and, for you (as a Board Member), 10+ hours of your life with which you could have been doing something more meaningful.

The opportunity to collectively discuss, debate and decide the future with some of the best, the brightest and the most dedicated community minds in the destination is powerful stuff. You have that ability if you have developed a Board of Destination Leaders.

In fact, I strongly believe you have that RESPONSIBILITY to your community. To not take this bull by the horns is akin to forfeiting your birthright. You are one of a select handful of people in your community who have been given a great gift... the chance to make a difference for your contemporaries, your children and your children's children.

There are few opportunities in life that afford us with such a chance to make a lasting difference in our communities. While it might happen on the Boards of Chambers of Commerce and may happen on the United Way Board, infrastructure projects that change the face of the community are more likely to emanate from DMO Boards.

This isn't meant as a shot at Chambers or the United Way or any other non-profit organization. They all exist to benefit their communities...and most are successful in improving the quality of life for their members or their clients. But these improvements are rarely permanent, destination-altering changes.

On the other hand, the Public Assembly Facilities, Downtown Revitalization projects, Waterfront Redevelopments and other Destination infrastructure improvements are lasting impacts. The Convention Center project in Madison changed the face of Wisconsin's Capitol City forever. A downtown left for dead in the early '90s has been transformed into a dining and entertainment hotspot. Over $500 million of private sector reinvestment has flooded into the downtown over the past decade. Community apathy and negativism has been replaced by an infectious "can-do" spirit. And, energized by the excitement of the Convention Center referendum win, a community-leader couple single-handedly established and funded the Overture Foundation to build a $200 million performing and visual arts center just off the Capitol Square. Had they not been involved with and inspired by the Convention Center project, I sincerely doubt that Madison would today be blessed with one of the finest cultural facilities in the United States.

All this...from a breakaway group of Destination Leaders that refused to buy-in to the old way of thinking. They ignored the hundreds of other "community leaders" that scoffed at the idea of trying to adapt a Frank Lloyd Wright design into a shoreline Convention Center. They changed the future of Madison.

Just as Destination Leaders have changed the face of Cleveland, Indianapolis, Providence, Dubuque and several cities all across North America. They were laughed at, too. But, they saw the opportunity to make a difference...and seized it.

So should you....

But...it's not only Destinational Enhancements that should power a DMO Board. Strengthening the organization is just as important.

Especially in these days of tightening governmental budgets, Destination Leaders need to focus their attention on an aggressive public information campaign in order to deflect potential raids upon the monies that have been historically invested in the DMO. It's the public support of the Board, outlining the negative consequences of a decrease in the DMO budget, resulting in a corresponding loss of jobs and tax revenue, that will be the most compelling to public officials.

In other destinations, the public information campaign will generate support for an increase in room tax investment in the DMO. Or maybe it's a portion of the local sales tax. Whatever it may be, the Board's voice here is one of painting a picture of opportunity, rather than warning of losses.

And, outside of building budgetary resources, Destination Leaders focus their attention on building a positive public image for the organization....not once, but every year. While a strong public persona will certainly help in building a competitive budget, it also goes a long way to paving the path for protecting your position and advancing your proposals.

Ever notice that individuals, businesses and organizations that are highly regarded tend to slice through the process like butter? By developing a positive public personality for the organization, Boards can pave the way for any number of initiatives...from building the budget to enhancing the infrastructure of the destination.

All this requires a Board that agrees it will not sit by and "oversee" or "review" the organization's work. It takes a Board that firmly agrees that it has work to do...and they're just the group of people to get it done!

CHAPTER 8

Developing Destination Influence

IF YOU'RE STILL WITH ME, you've taken a most powerful step. You've chosen the road less traveled...

It's about that 3 Degrees of Separation thing that we talked about in Chapter 5. It's time now to exercise the "juice" that you have...to turn relationships into power.

At your next Board Retreat (you *do* schedule an annual retreat, don't you?), take time out to identify the key "influencers" in your destination. List the individuals that score the most quotes in the media. The ones that seem to be on the invitation list at all the major events in the community. The ones that people either love or hate.

Once completed and prioritized, this "Touch List" should be divided among the Board, with each member taking names that they believe are appropriate

> *...you gotta be there before you gotta be there.*

matches. Bob could select Carol and Jose because they're all in Rotary (service club ties provide some of the best networking opportunities). Julie might select Melissa because she always sees her across the lobby when these two music lovers attend the symphony.

Look for common threads that allow you to connect and build rapport with these influencers. Don't play the DMO card right away. As the old lobbying adage goes, "you gotta be there *before* you gotta be there." Build a relationship upon which, if and when the time is right, you'll be able to segue into an exploratory conversation to learn their level of understanding and support of the hospitality industry, the DMO and your cause.

Several of the influencers on the Board's List will, no doubt, be politicians. And, while it pains us all to admit it, money talks. Campaign contributions earn you an ear with key politicians. Substantial campaign contributions can often earn you a politico's support.

Clearly, the DMO cannot make such contributions... and, as a general rule, the CEO should be extremely judicious when wading into this arena. Board members are the perfect contributors, especially if your Board roster is a diverse cross section of the community and cannot be pigeonholed as "those tourism people."

Even if you prefer not to engage in this strategy, the practice of political contribution holds another opportunity for building organizational influence. As the Board builds its "Touch List," be sure to include the top contributors to the most influential politicians in your destination. Contributor lists are public record and provide a tactical insight into who has the politician's ear.

If you can't get through to the Mayor, focus on his top contributors. Chances are they are business people who would be more likely to understand the importance of a competitively funded DMO and destination development. Make a successful case to them and they may be able to sway the Mayor (who would hate to disappoint one of his biggest contributors).

You don't hear the term "Power Lunches" much any-more...but they are still an effective strategy for building relationships that can pay off down the road. Given the hectic schedules of most of the people that qualify for "Touch List" status, getting 45 minutes of quality time with your target is virtually impossible.

Not so at lunch. Once the "Touch List" has been divided and assigned, decide how many lunches in a month you're willing to dedicate to building relationships on behalf of the DMO (and, if your list contains key influencers, remember that these relationship can also pay off for you *personally*). If your list is, say, 6 people deep and you're willing to spend two lunches a month on this strategy, that means you'll touch your list quarterly. Not a bad start for only 2 lunch-hours a month! And, if you're counting calories or carbs (or both), this works just as well over coffee.

...your Board should also have a visibility strategy.

Outside of the personal contact strategy, your Board should also have a visibility strategy. Board members should be seen at ribbon-cuttings, major news conferences, important city council meetings and community events. Your Board may even want to encourage its members to sit on other Boards to bring a destination eye to other organizations who may not be aware of the importance of a thriving tourism economy to *their* mission.

Your DMO may want to consider investing in profession-ally produced nametags for Board members so that they are, not only seen but, identified as being a Destination Leader. In time, these nametags will also produce an increased level of awareness and appreciation of the organization ("those guys are everywhere!").

Of course, the easiest path to such visibility is at DMO-sponsored events. Media Briefings* are the most effective because, by their very nature, they attract reporters by the score. Every DMO, regardless of the size of the destination, should hold at least 2 Media Briefings a year: One to announce the destination's prior year impact numbers each spring and the other to present awards to local residents that have "made a difference" in the community.

Other Media Briefings should be scheduled when there is a story worth talking about (and, be honest here...will Joe and Jill Public care?). Announcing a major convention or event win, the breaking of a record for Welcome Center visitors or developing a corporate partnership with a major credit card company would be reasons to consider staging a Press Briefing.

These are perfect opportunities for Board members to be seen by the media as destination leaders, integral to the economic vitality of the community. By appearing in public, you also reinforce the notion that the organization is far more than just the paid CEO...and that the organization has wide-spread business support. This is a subtle reminder to reporters that trying to develop a negative story line about the DMO may not be as easy as trying to develop dirt on an entity with less community muscle. With broad-based community leaders in attendance at your Media Briefings, reporters are forced to consider how the publisher or station owner will react if they try to dirty the reputation of business acquaintances and, more importantly, customers.

Of course, this strategy works even better if you have cultivated relationships with the owners, publishers and general managers of the region's media outlets. Just as the Board should

---

*FYI: TV and Radio types hate it when you call them "Press Conferences," as that connotes an event designed for print publications.

be insuring that there are regular performance and productivity reports being made to government, it should also be providing those reports to the owners and managers of local newspapers, radio, TV and magazines.

In the case of those outlets that offer opinion, schedule regular visits with the editorial board. Use the opportunity to educate these influencers on the importance of the industry and the DMO's role. Use the meetings to sound out these individuals on new initiatives you may be considering. After all, it sure would be nice to know whether the paper would aggressively oppose an increase in the restaurant tax before you propose it. And knowing that they would oppose such an initiative gives the Board the opportunity to massage the proposal into something more palatable.

Other opportunities for Board visibility could include the organization's Annual Meeting, Member/Partner events (such as "Business After Hours" style mixers and/or Member Educational Workshops) and any other time industry partners gather.

Achieving Destination Leadership involves working the 3 Degrees of Separation to your advantage. And, public visibility is a big part of that strategy.

There will be times when the Board needs to go beyond visibility and make a public statement. Maybe it's in support of a destination project. Maybe a reporter from the local *Business Journal* wants a statement from the Board on the progress in landing a new CEO. Whatever it may be, there will be times that the Board needs to make a statement. And, the Board must have a designated spokesperson to insure that the message being conveyed is the right one.

Often, this spokesperson is the Board Chair. In those situations where the Board Chair is uncomfortable in the media spotlight, another officer can be the designee. But, whoever it is, that individual should be well versed in both the activities of the DMO as well as how to handle reporters that are trolling for a story.

To be sure, your CEO (or *their* designee) may get most of the media requests on traditional topics like business levels, the economic impact of certain events and the like. However, on big destination and organizational issues, the voice of a business owner who has a stake in their community resonates more richly than the paid executive of a Destination Marketing Organization. Regardless of how convincing a communicator your CEO may be, that individual is often seen as a "hired-hand" from out of town. And, regardless of their love of and commitment to the community, there will always be some locals who see these paid executives as "carpetbaggers."

Of course, there are those times that the paid executive of the DMO is a *born* communicator. They can tap into the consciousness of a community and connect with the zeitgeist of the citizenry in the blink of an eye. And, in these situations, some Boards will take a public back seat, allowing the CEO to be the face and voice of the organization.

Such a strategy will likely produce strong short-term results. But sending the CEO out to champion a project or a cause is often a recipe for conflict down the road. Indeed, the smart CEO will often demure from the suggestion that they lead the charge, as they know the perils that await.

The need for some to be in the spotlight is an unfortunate trait of human nature. Oh, it's fine for those who choose a life in entertainment...but for the rest of us, it's rarely an attractive attribute. And for those who rarely get the chance to bask in the public spotlight they crave, jealousy often seeps into the equation.

When it comes time to take the bows after a successful destination win, the members of the Board of the DMO who led the charge should be in the front row. After all, these Board members were the ones who hatched and nurtured the concept, organized the support mechanism and brought the project home. Or did they?

A charismatic CEO may be seen by the media (and, thus, the community), as the shining star who "brought home the bacon." And when it's the paid executive whose picture is featured on the front page of the newspaper (and not a member of the DMO Board who, in their mind, worked just as hard on the project), the CEO-Board relationship can begin to take on a hint of envy.

> *...it's usually best if select members of the Board are also frequently seen as the public face and voice of the DMO...*

Some members of the Board may foolishly resent the accolades being directed to their executive. Despite the fact that the DMO got the job done, they'd prefer a bit more notoriety be directed toward themselves. Thus, even with a charismatic CEO, it's usually best if select members of the Board are also frequently seen as the public face and voice of the DMO...and the effort.

Finally, some of the initiatives you may have chosen as Strategic Goals may carry with them a degree of danger. Supporting an initiative that the Mayor hates. Advocating a tax increase to build a Public Assembly Facility. Supporting a plan that will locate a new Headquarters Hotel next to the Convention Center when occupancy rates throughout the city are hovering at 50%.

Never mind that all these projects may be desperately needed in the destination. These are the kinds of initiatives that may incur a vicious political or community backlash, toasting the DMO in the public eye.

A word to the wise: Don't send your CEO out alone to advocate for these types of projects. If there is danger in the air, you run the risk of sacrificing your paid executive on a project that requires a coordinated, well-populated offensive as well as defensive plan. Regardless of how good he is, you'll end up diminishing his future effectiveness if he is the one who takes all the arrows.

If the initiative carries an inherent degree of danger, the Board should take the lead. That's one of the reasons you are there.

CHAPTER 9

Leaving a Mark

YOU'VE ESTABLISHED YOUR PRESENCE. You've communicated your worth. Now, it's time to select the mark.

Chances are, you already know what the destination needs. It's been talked about in the papers, at service club lunches and discussed with friends over golf or drinks. It's a new or expanded Convention Center. It's a new Sports Complex. It's an entertainment district downtown. It's revitalizing the waterfront. It's developing a new "destination attraction." It's...well, you probably already know what "IT" is.

If you don't...it's time for a Board Retreat to decide. It might even be time for a stakeholder or community survey to gauge partner and public interest in what the next big thing should be. Or, you might consider researching the customer on what *they* think

...a destination that isn't pursuing the "next big thing" is a destination in decline.

would make your destination even better. Regardless of how you go about gathering intelligence, research data is crucial in your efforts to make the right decisions on behalf of the destination.

Ultimately, you'll identify new initiatives to be pursued. If you don't, look again. Because a destination that isn't pursuing the "next big thing" is a destination in decline.

It doesn't necessarily have to be bricks and mortar development. It could be an initiative to increase the organization's budget. It could be the development of a program to attract, train and deploy a quality hospitality workforce. It could be leading the hospitality industry out of its traditional "What, Me Vote?" malaise into a political juggernaut.

But it has to be something...or you will lose the best and brightest from your ranks (because the best and the brightest want to be involved in something meaningful). You'll risk political support if they don't see a vital and active organization. And you'll forfeit business community support if they can't see an organization dedicated to enhancing the economic climate of the region.

But how to choose? That depends (again) on you and the needs and culture of your destination. All we can suggest is that, whatever you select, it passes this 5 point test.

1) Will it benefit a super majority (at least 67%) of your members or industry partners?

2) Will the initiative make the destination more attractive among its "competitive set"?*

3) Will the initiative strengthen the organization in either public/political awareness, appreciation and support and/or by increasing its budgetary resources?

* *"Competitive Set:" the destinations or DMOs with which the organization traditionally competes for business. While usually geographic in nature, some competitive sets may include destinations of similar population, DMO budget size, convention center square footage or sports facility inventory.*

4) Will it improve the quality of life for areas residents by attracting visitor spending to the area?

5) Will it help create jobs for the community?

The more "Yes" answers you can honestly give to these questions, the more likely that you have found your "IT." If you are in the enviable position of having a number of "IT" possibilities clustered at the top of the list, we offer two diverse tie-breakers for your consideration:

1) Is there a better than even chance of success?

2) Will your kids be proud of you for being involved in the project?

First question first. If you have one "IT" project, it doesn't matter much what the chances of success are (unless it's zero). You have no other choice but to pursue the initiative.

However, if you are blessed with a number of possible directions in which to direct your influence (and there is no clear-cut "IT" already planted in the mind of the Mayor), it is often best to choose the path of least resistance.

Will it help create jobs for the community?

Going for the brass ring and missing on your first try at significant destination leadership isn't the end of the world...but it doesn't position you well for your second attempt. On the other hand, knocking down a couple of easier wins in short succession positions you smartly for an assault on a bigger target. Thus, unless there is a compelling reason to choose one of the hardest initiatives first, a smart Board will gain experience and momentum by shooting smaller in its initial forays into Destination Leadership.

So, set your sights. Choose your mark. It's your time.

CHAPTER 10

Accountability, Transparency & Ethics

AS DON HENLEY SANG on his first solo album, *"We love to cut you down to size. We love dirty laundry."*

After years of trying to get the news media to recognize the DMO industry, it has finally happened...but for all the wrong reasons.

We thought we had a compelling story to tell. Visitors pay a tax that, in most cases, residents don't. That tax is invested in a DMO to attract more visitors. Those visitors spend millions of dollars in our community, creating jobs, enabling new entrepreneurial business starts and adding additional tax revenue to local government. Government is able to increase the services residents expect without increasing property taxes. What a story!

Instead, we're also getting noticed for all the wrong things. In a number of major markets (and a few whistlestops), DMOs were drawn and quartered and their CEOs sent packing for what was considered "lavish" spending or questionable business decisions. A few have suffered through embarrassing embezzlement cases. Others for personal missteps of high-profile CEOs.

While embezzlement and conflict of interest rightfully deserve to be reported, many of the stories made it to prime time because the media smelled a story that it could exploit...and, it could exploit the story because most people don't understand what DMOs do. And some people are just jealous of the lives they *think* CVB professionals live.

But, that's the hand that you, as a Destination Leader, have been dealt. And, as we discussed in Chapter 8, you should be cultivating relationships with the publishers and station managers of local media outlets to try to slow these kind of uninformed attacks from even getting out of the assignment editor's mouth.

However, you must understand that it is not just the media's fault. As long as your organization is the recipient of any kind of funding from government, you run the risk of taking your turn under the microscope. And, in today's rapid-fire, sound-byte powered media world, the words "tax," "benefits," "entertainment" and "private" will position you as "guilty before being proved innocent," as was the case in many of the cities where CVBs were targeted. And, once presumed guilty, the organization is in a world of hurt.

So, dealt this hand of useless cards, what is the Destination Leader to do? In short, buy a big copy machine and an even bigger mirror. The copy machine is for all the statistics and reports you'll be printing for government officials, the media and local community leaders. The mirror is for looking at your organization's practices on a regular basis.

The importance of regular reporting to the community cannot be overstated. At the very least, these reports should be quarterly. At best, monthly. And they don't have to be long...a couple of pages will do. After all, most of the people who receive them won't have the time to actually read them. At the same time, some will...so don't go filling them with fluff.

The critical importance is not, however, whether they read these documents...it's that they receive regular, open communication from the organization. The very presence of these reports in their mailbox each month says:

- We have an exciting story to tell that you should be excited to hear

- Our work is important enough to the community that you need to know about it

- We have nothing to hide

The organization that relies *only* upon a glossy annual report is begging for scrutiny. Annual reports look too perfect. Many annual reports look expensive ("is THIS what they're using tax dollars on?"). Many annual reports only touch the recipient once a year. That gives those that might want to develop a story the other 364 days to ask, "what have you done for me lately."

And that's where it usually starts. Most DMO meltdowns begin with a well-placed innuendo.

- "I saw the CEO out to dinner at the most expensive restaurant in town."

- "So, I hear the whole sales staff is attending a trade show in Vegas. Isn't that convenient?"

- "Do you know what the DMO is doing to market the new Convention Center? No? Hmmmm, neither do we."

Notice how none of these statements are an outright indictment of wrong-doing? The CEO in question was out to dinner with his parents, celebrating their 40th anniversary (and, his parents were buying).

The two sales people that make up the "whole sales staff" were attending the trade show because the DMO had strategically selected this new, growing niche market as a prime target in its annual marketing plan. And, located in Vegas, it gave them a chance to call on two clients that were considering bringing six events to town at an estimated economic impact of $3.4 million over the next three years.

And, the person asking about what the DMO was doing to market the new Convention Center? That was the Board Chair of the Downtown Merchants Association trying to rile a Mayor into shifting the room tax from the DMO to the DMA. Notice that he didn't say the DMO *wasn't* marketing the Convention Center. He didn't say the DMO was doing a bad job. He just asked if the Mayor knew the plan, knowing that Mayors hate being in the dark on anything. And the sinister, "hmmm?," was all the innuendo he needed to launch the Mayor into orbit.

I know...because it happened to me. The Mayor and I had become friends. After doing everything but ride a unicycle naked down State Street to convince him of the importance of the DMO and tourism in general, we had built a relationship that benefited both of us. But, like many friends, I had gotten lazy and had left him out of the loop on the marketing plan for the new center.

Not that he needed to know. He didn't really care. He knew I had a talented staff and a hot agency working tirelessly on marketing the center. But when someone drops an innuendo... people perk up their ears and start sniffing for a scandal. And he was no different as he picked up the phone and barked, "My office. Now."

I learned a valuable lesson that day. So did the Downtown Merchants Association, as the Mayor lit up their proposal like the 4th of July for trying to play the two of us off against each other for their own gain. But, when somebody wants something...innuendo is a powerfully effective tool. Copious reporting and communication is the only known antidote to innuendo. And that's why we recommend lots of data in lots of reports on lots of occasions. Nobody can say they didn't know (or that we didn't try to tell them).

While serving as the Chairman of DMAI, Atlanta CVB CEO Spurgeon Richardson coined the phrase, "Accountability and Transparency." That we need to be accountable is, of course, abundantly clear. We need to, at all times and in all places, communicate our ROI to our community, stakeholders and elected leaders.

...even if you have law on your side, you look guilty as sin if you try to hide behind it.

The "Transparency" aspect, however, is foreign to many DMOs. As non-profit 501(c)(6) organizations, many DMOs are private entities. And, as such, most are not *legally* compelled to open their books to government or media requests.

However, if a request is made by government or the media to review your books, program of work or sales productivity statistics, Richardson's "Transparency" mantra should trump any legal considerations. Because, even if you have law on your side, you *look* guilty as sin if you try to hide behind it. And, instantly, you will lose all the good will you've built over the years. Chances are you're not guilty...but you'll sure look it.

And that brings us to the mirror.

During the spate of DMO meltdowns, it was discovered that the sales personnel of one CVB had expensed client entertainment at strip clubs. Now, one could say that there is nothing wrong with this. After all, the strip club was a Bureau member in good standing. Going to a strip club is not illegal. And the client is worth $10 million to the city. He wants to go to a strip club? He goes.

There were a number of reasons that the CEO and Chairman of the CVB Board ultimately resigned. But ask Joe and Jill Public what they remember about the DMO, and they'll say "strip clubs."

Playing Monday Morning Quarterback is easy...but here's a test that could have saved this CVB a lot of tears:

- Would I want my 13-year old daughter to know that I go to strip clubs?

- Would my mother be proud of me?

- What would my biggest enemy do with this information?

- How would this look on the front page of the paper or on the evening News?

These four questions can be applied in most situations as "the mirror" that every DMO should hold up to review its every decision.

At one of the CVBs that ended up being crucified by the media, the real issue boiled down to padding sales productivity numbers. Would their parents have been proud of them for lying on a report to make a few thousand dollars more in bonuses? Doubtful.

At another, a local newspaper and a TV station teamed up to investigate what *they* believed to be lavish spending on the part of Bureau personnel. Never mind that the Board had approved virtually every expense in question. The media knew that it could make some of these expenses look incriminating. And they did it with innuendo:

"While you were making Hamburger Helper for dinner, Bureau staff dined on fois gras and champagne..."

The CEO was toast within days. His Board put him on paid leave (essentially accusing him of mismanagement), called for an audit and went underground for the next few months. By the time the audit came back clean, the City and County were already discussing whether to form their own DMO and discontinue funding the CVB. The Convention Center proposal that was advancing slowly through the public discourse was DOA. And the accounting and legal bills cost taxpayers hundreds of thousands of dollars.

Should this DMO staff and Board have used a mirror? Of course. The now ex-CEO of the Bureau himself says that the $1000 golf outings and some of his perks, like dual country club memberships, were asking for trouble.

So was buying thousands of dollars of seats to the city's major league baseball club's games. While the seats were for entertaining clients (what a great way to spend quality time with people who can bring business to your town), there were days when there were no clients available to entertain. On those days, staff and Board got to use the tickets. But how do you think that's going to play in the papers? Joe and Jill Public can't afford a ticket to the game and yet "their tax dollars" are being used to send a bunch of Bureau people out to the ballpark? Not a story that generates a lot of support for the home team, is it?

Using the mirror and asking the four questions will go a long way towards removing your DMO from the line of fire. But, whether it's hubris or an old-fashioned case of over-justification, DMOs can still find themselves on the defensive. Especially today, as Television News outlets across the country mimic each other in an attempt at winning the ratings sweeps.

So, what does a Destination Leader do when the media comes knocking? If you've created strong operating and conduct policies, been reporting aggressively to your stakeholders, building relationships throughout the community and holding an internal mirror up to your organization...you stand up, answer the questions truthfully, admit what you don't know that they may have dug up and pledge to get back to them with more answers, pronto.

If you sandbag them, dance around the truth, say "no comment," look nervous or say "we don't have to reveal those numbers," you're in for a rocky ride. Because, like wild animals, newspeople can sense when you're scared and the scent of blood in the water is a powerful aphrodisiac.

I've often believed that Bill Clinton could have skated past the lion's share of the Monica Lewinsky scandal by simply telling the truth. Hey, he could have even lied the first time that he was asked about his relationship with the intern. But when it was clear that he was caught, he could have ended the majority of the controversy by saying, "I lied because I didn't want my 17-year old daughter to think I was a schmuck."

> **If you sandbag them, dance around the truth, say "no comment," look nervous or say "we don't have to reveal those numbers," you're in for a rocky ride.**

While Americans still should have been outraged...most would have given him a day pass on this issue because, with that explanation, we could understand what could have made him lie. In the same situation, we might have done the same thing for the same reason. And, interestingly, we're right back to the "what would my daughter think of my behavior" test.

In the case of the Bureau that placed their CEO on administrative leave, the Board and the organization would have been better served by the Board Chairman responding to the allegations of inappropriate spending of tax dollars by first explaining the role of the CVB in generating millions of dollars of tax revenues for the City and the County. In a perfect world, the statement would have sounded something like this:

"Over the past eight years, your CVB has generated over $245 million in tax revenues, a ROI of 14:1 for the room tax revenues that have been entrusted in this organization during that time. In other words, we've saved the average property taxpayer in the County $125 each year by getting visitors to foot the bill and we've helped create over 4,000 new jobs. We've done it with an aggressive sales and marketing program that has made this city one of the top convention destinations in the Midwest, despite the lack of a competitive convention center.

"Recent news reports have suggested that the Bureau has been spending money inappropriately in this endeavor to enhance the economy of the County. We appreciate the concerns that have been raised but caution the public from jumping to conclusions. The Board of Directors of this organization has been aware of and approved many of the expenditures that have been questioned by reporters who may not understand how unique and highly competitive this business is. We have several policy and expenditure controls in place to prevent misappropriation of funds. This is not an organization that is running amok.

"However, we can understand how some of these allegations might look to those who don't understand how destinations compete for business or how organizations retain a quality workforce. While we have often measured ourselves against our peer organizations across the country, we are, today, keenly aware that there is another test we should be applying to our work...and that is how you, our most important client, views our way of doing business.

"If you don't believe that the CVB should be supporting our major league teams by buying a block of tickets to use when entertaining clients when they are in town, then this organization should reconsider this practice next year. But, I gotta tell you, we've booked some major pieces of business for this city at these games, golf outings and dinners at the city's finest restaurants. And, during our CEO's tenure, this City has rocked the competition.

"In order to insure that we are investing room tax dollars effectively and appropriately, the CVB will be engaging an outside firm to review our practices and policies and make recommendations on how we can do an even better job. We anticipate that this process should take no more than 45 days and, while the CVB is a private corporation, we will be pleased to share the findings of this report with you along with our plans to make the CVB even more effective and accountable than ever before.

"We stand behind our President 100% and believe that the City is best served with him continuing to focus his attention on booking more business for our city while the outside audit proceeds...."

To recap the strategy just played:

- Come out strong and proud by stating the impacts that the organization has made and that the destination has enjoyed

- Acknowledge the accusations

- Suggest that the allegations are founded on faulty assumptions by those who may not have a complete understanding of the industry

- Quickly agree that you can see how people could be concerned

- Reaffirm that the Board is "on the case" and takes these concerns seriously

- Suggest a possible change to placate critics...but caution that the ultimate results may not be what they want

- Announce a full and rapid review, pledging public disclosure

- Finish strong by supporting the CEO and suggesting that the CVB needs to get back to work on behalf of the people in the destination

For Board Members that are uncomfortable with coming out strong and supporting your CEO, I have to ask, "why?" Unless you already know that he has been playing fast and loose with budget and policies (in which case, the fault here lies fully with the Board for not dealing with this issue before it blew up in the media), why wouldn't you support him?

Hanging your CEO out to dry hurts the organization and makes the Board look bad. If it turns out that the CEO *was* at fault, you have the opportunity to can him after the audit. If he wasn't at fault, and you put him on leave, you've lost a destination professional, months of effective leadership and the likelihood that he'll be moving on soon after the dust settles (wouldn't you?).

Unless there is a clear-cut violation of policy and ethics, time is on the Board's side. Firing or putting a CEO on leave only makes the Board look decisive...not right. And, frankly, decisive doesn't count for that much. At the risk of using another sports metaphor, nobody really cares that the winning team scored 35 unanswered points in the first period. When people look back after a few years, they'll only remember that the team won.

The days of DMOs living life in a fishbowl have just begun.

It's the same here. Destination Leaders don't try to look good by being decisive. Destination Leaders look good by being professional, thoughtful and fair. If the CEO is found to have violated policy or ethics, the media may childishly chant, "told ya so," but the Board can score even more points by responding, "thank you for uncovering this." No one will think less of the Board for admitting a mistake if it corrects it when the flaw is proven. In fact, many will think more highly of a group that handles such issues in such a measured fashion.

And then, there is the issue of conflict of interest. A number of DMOs have recently come under political and media fire for doing business with Board Members. Even if the Board Member is providing the product or service at a rate that is far below market expectations, this practice just doesn't look good. If you, as a Board Member, wish to do business with your DMO, prudence suggests that you step off the Board.

And, finally, there is the issue of the Board speaking with one voice. We've seen several cases of individuals publicly opposing Board positions on Destination Development and Room Tax Allocation. In one case, a Board Member went so far as to question the capability of his Bureau's CEO.

Part of the ethical fabric of a DMO Board is that minority-view voices do not speak to the media. While the Board Member may be right that the CEO doesn't have what it takes to lead the organization, the media is no place to make such a suggestion. For now, the reputation of the organization is on the line. Governmental and community leaders will assume the Bureau isn't being managed properly. Maybe they'll decide to reallocate funds away from the Bureau. And then, the Bureau will really struggle to have the impact that this Board Member expects.

If any member of the Board does harm to the organization, it is that organization's duty to remove him from the Board.

The days of DMOs living life in a fishbowl have just begun. Transparency and Accountability are crucial to our future survival. If you haven't adopted a Professional Code of Ethics or Conduct, do so in the next couple of meetings. The DMAI Code (found on the following page) is a great start. At your next Board Meeting, form a Board Task Force to review and, if appropriate, enhance the Code to meet your standards. Then discuss, massage and adopt it at the next meeting.

Then live by it...and the mirror.

DMAI STANDARDS OF CONDUCT

The DMAI Executive Committee recommends that the Board of Directors support the association's efforts, on behalf of the convention and visitors bureaus industry to adopt a standards guideline. The standards of conduct will reinforce the need and demand for greater transparency and accountability within the profession.

The recommended standards are as follows:

1. Maintain loyalty to the bureau that employs me and discharge your responsibilities with dedication to achieving the objectives of your bureau.

2. Actively encourage the integration of ethics into all aspects of management of the bureau activities.

3. Uphold all laws, regulations, and operating policies relating to your bureau.

4. Serve all constituents of your bureau impartially, and to provide no special privilege to any individual constituent, nor to accept special personal compensation from an individual constituent, except with the knowledge and consent of your governing stakeholders.

5. Comply with all levels of governmental regulations concerning lobbying and political activities and to use only legal, ethical and moral means when attempting to influence legislation or regulations affecting your bureau or the convention and visitor industry.

Continued on next page

6. Issue no false or deliberately misleading statements or advertisements concerning your bureau or community, any other bureau or community, or the convention and visitor industry to the media, the public or any other persons, either affiliated with or unrelated to the convention and visitor industry.

7. Actively encourage diversity through the inclusion of qualified people from diverse backgrounds including but not limited to women, ethnic, racial minorities, and refuse to engage in and or sanction discrimination on the basis of race, gender, age religion, national origin, sexual orientation, physical appearance, or disability.

8. Refuse to engage in and or sanction activities for personal gain at the expense of the bureau, which employs me.

9. Build collaborative relationships with other bureau industry professionals and others for the advancement of the profession of destination management.

10. Acceptance as a member of DMAI implies that you fully understand and agree to the terms of the Code of Professional Conduct. Adherence to this Code assures those associated with the convention and visitor industry that DMAI members and their staff constantly strive to achieve and maintain the highest standards of professionalism and integrity. Deliberate and intentional violation could subject you to censure and possible suspension.

CHAPTER 11

YOU ARE A DESTINATION LEADER.

You have already displayed a rare level of commitment to this role and your community by completing this book. There are a myriad of things you could have been doing with these past couple hours...but you chose to enhance your understanding of one of the most misunderstood industries in the world. And, one of the most critical industries to our intricate economy.

If the days after 9/11 didn't demonstrate the importance of travel to the world's economy, I'm not sure what will. So, we need to know that our work as Destination Leaders will often be dismissed as low impact, chided as supporting low wage jobs and attacked for wasting tax dollars.

In many communities, we are still years away from being an automatic consideration for inclusion on any Task Force or Commission that is created to look at future development needs. In other communities, residents will view visitors with disdain, ignorant of the value they bring, not just in their wallets but also in the sharing of culture, diversity, ideas and friendship.

Destination Leadership can be a lonely, frustrating path to follow. But, as our parents surely told us, the most important things in life are never the easiest. And there is no nobler a role in our community than Destination Leader.

For those who arch a skeptical eyebrow at such a bold statement, consider the "food chain" of every noble concern in our community. The Homeless? The Environment? Establishing Living Wage? Where does the money come from to power these concerns? Where is the sustainability for these programs?

When we were debating the opponents of Madison's Monona Terrace Convention Center in the early '90s, we used to wait eagerly for the accusation that this was bad public policy because convention centers only spawned low-wage, no-benefit jobs. Beyond the fact that such a statement is patently false, it gave us the opportunity to suggest that it was the opponents of the projects who were "elitist" for opposing job creation for those under-educated and unemployed in our city. This was the sector of the community that was most in need of assistance...and an enhanced hospitality base would create opportunities for hundreds to get off public assistance programs and out of homeless shelters every year.

Today, instead of fighting for a share of the room tax dollars traditionally invested in the DMO, the Executive Director of Madison's Transitional Housing organization credits the Greater Madison Convention & Visitors Bureau as one of his agency's biggest partners in creating opportunities for his clients to earn a living wage and afford their own housing.

In the book *Accept Your Abundance*, author Randy Gage offers the somewhat Ayn Rand-ian viewpoint that he can have a bigger impact on those less fortunate by becoming sensationally wealthy. Sure, he could volunteer in a soup kitchen once or twice a month. But, if he used that time to increase his wealth to a level where he could actually employ one or two of the people getting their meals from the soup kitchen, he will have had a far more profound impact on the community.

As Destination Leaders, we can enhance our community by creating an organization that is rock solid, professionally staffed, universally respected in the destination and has a competitive budget. This type of an organization will create economic impact, increase tax revenues back to the City, County and State and will create new jobs and business start-ups.

We can also enhance our community by aggressively advocating for destination developments. From a public assembly facility to downtown revitalization to waterfront enhancements, anything that makes the destination more attractive to visitors will enhance the quality of life for residents. They may not understand how a convention center can benefit their lives but they'll surely appreciate the new dining, retail and entertainment nightspots that pop up around the facility.

And, those new destination enhancements will go a long way to making the community attractive to young professionals. If you're familiar with the book *Rise of the Creative Class* by Richard Florida, you know that smart communities are focusing on ways to attract young talent instead of building industrial parks or forking over incentive checks to lure companies to town. As former HP CEO Carly Fiorina told the National Governors Association in 2000, "Keep your tax incentives and highway interchanges; we will go where the highly skilled people are."

What this all means is that the tide is turning for Destination Leaders when it comes to infrastructure development. If the "traditional" economic development types are buying into Florida's research and recommendations, we're finally in a position to agree on many of the types of developments that should be pursued. After all, outside of Convention Centers and Stadiums (which Florida doesn't see as vital to attracting young talent), most destination development that attracts visitors *will* attract young talent. And everybody wins.

Look around your community. Count the number of organizations that can have the impact that your DMO can have on the long-term viability of your town. Chances are, you'll use one hand and have fingers to spare.

Take your job seriously. You've been given quite a gift. Now, it's time to "just do it." Your community and its children, whether they know it or not, are counting on you.

Bill Geist
October 2007

EXHIBIT A

Industry Abbreviations & Acronyms

ABA: American Bus Association

ACME: Association of Convention Marketing Executives

ACOM: Association of Convention Operation Managers

ACTE: Association of Corporate Travel Executives

ADI: Area of Dominant Influence (used to determine media markets)

ADR: Average Daily Rate (a measure of hotel profitability)

ASAE: American Society of Association Executives, and host to one of the largest convention industry trade shows in North America

ASTA: American Society of Travel Agents

BID: Business Improvement District

CAE: Certified Association Executive

Carrying Capacity: The number of visitors that can adequately be accommodated with existing infrastructure such as lodging, dining, roads, parking, etc.

CDME: Certified Destination Marketing Executive

CIC: Convention Industry Council. An umbrella association for convention industry associations

CMP: Certified Meeting Professional

Consumer Show: Differs from a "Trade Show" as a trade show generally targets industry professionals. Consumer Shows target the consumer.

Conversion: Closing the sale

CSAE: Canadian Society of Association Executives.

CSM: Convention Services Manager

Cultural Tourism: Travel for the purpose of learning about the culture or heritage or an area

CVA: Convention & Visitors Association

CVB: Convention & Visitors Bureau

CTC: Certified Travel Counselor (also the Canadian Tourism Commission)

Day visitors: Visitors who arrive and leave the same day (also known as "Daytrippers")

DMAI: Destination Marketing Association International (the Trade Association for the DMO industry, formerly know as the International Association of Convention & Visitors Bureaus)

DMAP: Destination Marketing Accreditation Program

DMC: Destination Management Company (usually private sector)

DMO: Destination Marketing (or Management) Organization (usually non-profit or public sector)

EDC: Economic Development Council (or Corporation)

ESSTO : Educational Seminar for State Travel Officials

FAM / Familiarization Trip: A complimentary or reduced-rate travel program for travel writers, group tour operators, travel agents, airline or rail employees or other travel buyers, designed to acquaint participants with specific destinations or suppliers and to stimulate the sale of travel.

FIT: Foreign independent traveler (or Fully Independent Traveler)

Fulfillment Piece: Promotional literature, video or other material that is sent in response to an inquiry

GLAMER: Group Leaders of America

HSMAI: Hospitality Sales and Management Association International

IAAM: International Association of Assembly Managers

IAAPA: International Association of Amusement Parks & Attractions

IACC: International Association of Conference Centers

IAEM: International Association of Exposition Managers

ICCA: International Congress and Convention Association

IFEA: International Festivals and Events Association

Incentive Tour: A trip offered as a prize, usually by a company to stimulate employee sales or productivity

Interpretation: Print materials, signage, narration, guided tours and anything that "interprets" the site or destination for the visitor.

ITME: Incentive Travel and Meetings Expo

Leisure Visitor: Leisure tourists, in contrast with business travelers, travel for pleasure and thus are not under any obligations to frequent specific destinations or facilities.

M&C: Meetings and Conventions

MPI: Meeting Professionals International

MTWA: Midwest Travel Writers Association

NASC: National Association of Sports Commissions

NAEM: National Association of Exposition Managers

NCBMP: National Coalition of Black Meeting Planners

NSA: National Speakers Association

NTA: National Tour Association

Occupancy rate: Percent of available hotel rooms sold during a particular span of time

PCMA: Professional Convention Management Association

Pow Wow: A Trade Show for the Group (Motorcoach) Travel Market, attended by operators and destinations from around the world

PRSA: Public Relations Society of America

Rack Card: The typical tourism brochure (sized 4" x 9") and used primarily in tourism racks.

Rack Rate: The official cost or a room posted by a hotel (but rarely paid by groups)

RCMA: Religious Conference Management Association

Receptive Operator: Someone who plans to "receive" a motor-coach or tour group. They may plan lodging, meals, attraction visits, etc. for a fee or commission

RevPar: Revenue per Available Room (a hotel performance measure)

RFP: Request for Proposal

RFQ: Request for Qualifications

ROI: Return on Investment

SATW: Society of American Travel Writers

SGMP: Society of Government Meeting Planners

SITE: Society of Incentive and Travel Executives

SMERF: A segment of the Convention & Meeting Market that stands for Social, Military, Educational, Religious and Fraternal.

STAR Report: A measurement (by Smith Travel Research) of hotel performance

Step-on Guide: A highly knowledgeable guide who "steps-on" an incoming motorcoach and provides narrative interpretation for the passengers

TDA: Tourism Development Authority

TDC: Tourism Development Council / Commission

TIA: Travel Industry Association of America

TIF: Tax Incremental Financing

TODS: Tourist Oriented Directional Signage (often the blue signs along interstates and highways

TOT: Transient Occupancy Tax (or "Room Tax")

Trade Show: A product showcase for a specific industry that is generally not open to the public.

TTRA: Travel and Tourism Research Association

USTOA: United States Tour Operators Association

VCB: Visitors and Convention Bureau

VFR: Visiting friends and relatives

VIC: Visitor Information Center (or Welcome Center)

Wayfinding Signage: Signs to aid the traveling public in finding their way around a destination

WTM: World Travel Market

WTO: World Tourism Organization

WTTC: World Travel and Tourism Council

About the Author

BILL GEIST consults destination marketing organizations around the globe and speaks to thousands each year on trends, marketing, legislative advocacy, destination development and the Internet.

As the former President of the Greater Madison (WI) Convention & Visitors Bureau, Bill was intimately involved in the campaign to build the Frank Lloyd Wright-designed Monona Terrace Convention Center. That project forever changed the face of Wisconsin's Capital City and spurred over $500 million in private sector reinvestment in the downtown in the decade since its opening.

Bill is the founder and host of the innovative distance learning series of teleseminars entitled DMOU (Destination Marketing Organization University) in which he interviews the best and the brightest names in Destination Marketing. You can view the entire audio catalogue at www.DMOU.com. He is also a contributor to the textbook *Fundamentals of Destination Marketing*.

You can learn more about Bill, his consulting and speaking offerings, his client newsletters and blog...and more on the Destination Leadership Series at the following websites:

www.ZeitgeistConsulting.com
www.BillGeist.com
www.DMOU.com
www.DestinationLeadership.com